Finding Favor

Dr. Chris Stephens

ACKNOWLEDGMENTS

"You surround him with favor as with a shield."
– Psalm 5:12

I'm so grateful it blows my mind! I definitely see God's favor at work through those who surround and shield me.

There is no such thing as a self-made person, nor is there a successful person who became so alone. I am no exception. God has blessed me with so many faithful friends, family, and staff I cannot possibly name them all for their years of pouring into me and making me who I am today. Forgive me for giving shout-outs to only a few.

First to Michele, my wife and better half, who encourages me daily. She is a constant support and force who pushes me. Love you 'Shey.' (That's what her dad calls her.)

To my kids, who are my first ministry and such a huge part of the ministry of Faith Promise.

To the staff of Faith Promise, who provided proofing, designing, editing, and incredible personal stories to motivate you in seeing and walking in God's favor.

To my assistant, Jody Kenyon, who keeps my life straight and gives wisdom and counsel beyond belief.

To my researcher, Drew Wells, who is a champion wordsmith and does more for me and Faith Promise than anyone realizes.

To my right hand of almost 20 years, Dr. Josh Whitehead, who pushes me to continue to write and add value to more people than I could have ever imagined.

Blessed is the man who has friends and traveling companions. Because of these and so many others, you hold a tool that will transform your life into what our Father desires for you.

It's incredible to live an Ephesians 3:20 life!

TABLE OF CONTENTS

Letter from Pastor Chris...7

Introduction 9

Day 1: The Source 15

Day 2: Perspective 20

Day 3: Gifts...24

Day 4: Mountains 29

Day 5: Words..34

Day 6: Connections 39

Day 7: Open Doors...44

Day 8: Signet Ring..50

Day 9: Cosmic Trials...54

Day 10: Out Of The Blue..59

Day 11: Set Apart..64

Day 12: Glorify God 68

Day 13: Heavy Glory..73

Day 14: Real People...78

Day 15: Real Problems..83

Day 16: Impossible 88

Day 17: Insecurity 93

Day 18: Walls of Protection 99

Day 19: In The Fire 104

Day 20: Keys 109

Day 21: Qualified 115

Day 22: Blessings 120

Day 23: Dreams 124

Day 24: Rise 129

Day 25: Majority 134

Day 26: What Are The Odds? 139

Day 27: Dream Again 144

Day 28: Jehovah-Jireh 150

Day 29: Jehovah-Rapha 155

Day 30: Jehovah-Sabaoth 161

Day 31: Jehovah-Shammah 166

Hey Promisor!

In the name of Jesus, this year will be your best year yet! After a year like 2020, this may be tough to hear, but it is essential for each of us to receive if we're going to see God's favor at work in our lives.

Now when I write the word "favor," I'm talking about a Holy Spirit-filled force at work in the life of every Christ follower. And I am convinced the Lord's design and desire is to pour out His favor on us. So, I challenge you to open your mind and heart, and commit to His work of growing up in Christ.

While writing this book, I was also preparing another, *Venture,* which you will hopefully read later this year, on how to develop a Personal Growth Plan. In it is an assessment to help you build a plan for your spiritual growth. I truly believe we will experience a more fulfilling and lasting walk with the Lord when we invite God to work in us and through us.

Also, I pray you've picked a defining word for the year. If you're not sure what that means, ask yourself this: what area in my life needs to grow so that this year will be my most exceptional year? That's your word! Once you've picked a word, ask the Lord daily to pour out His favor on your word for the year and ask your family, group, and friends to pray with you!

Lastly, let me challenge you to get in on the Faith Promise Bible reading plan with me this year. If you already have a plan to go and grow in God's Word, great! If you DON'T have a plan, I like my plan better than yours!

While you're at it, download the YouVersion Bible App to start the *Finding Favor* video devotional. It's a great way to get the content of this book in a video format you can watch, share, and go through with friends. If videos aren't your thing, *Finding Favor* is also available in audiobook and e-book format so you can consume it in the way you like best. Check out my website drchrisstephens.com for links to all the formats.

Please know I pray for you daily. I believe God is working in your life and calling you to enter into His presence, enjoy His blessings, and walk in His favor. And if you're still unsure how to see God's favor at work—that's what Finding Favor is all about!

> *Finding Favor* is also available in audiobook and e-book format so you can consume it in the way you like best.

Together let's seek out in faith and walk out in favor this incredible adventure!

Love,
Your Pastor

INTRODUCTION

There is no question we all want God's favor. And we want God to do today what the psalmist asked God to do thousands of years ago...

Let the favor of the Lord our God be upon us;
And confirm for us the work of our hands;
Yes, confirm the work of our hands.
– Psalm 90:17

Because God is always working, His favor is always at work. The only question is, will you look for it? This is why our theme this year will be finding favor and why over the next month we'll dive into how to do just that. His favor can make a miraculous difference in your life and walk with Jesus.

In **Ecclesiastes 9:10, the wisest king in human history under God's inspiration charged us: "Whatever your hand finds to do, do it with all your might."** To accomplish this, we need His favor on the work of our hands. The word favor appears 116 times in the Bible and there are many synonyms used for the word.

Favor is dripping from every page of Scripture.

Favor is a mark that sets followers of Christ apart.

But favor is far more than positive thinking.

Favor is a lifestyle the Lord wants us to soak up, soak in, and pour out on others. The Bible is saturated with admonitions about His favor. Luke, one of the earliest disciples, reminds us, **"And Jesus kept increasing in wisdom and stature, and in favor with God and men." – Luke 2:52**

Why can't we see an increase in favor, just like our Lord, Master, and Model?

By His grace and for His glory, I believe we can! My life is marked by an over-flowing of favor, because I know from experience how God is **"able to do far more abundantly beyond all that we ask or think, according to the power that works within us." – Ephesians 3:20**

Do you see God at work? Do you see yourself as blessed and favored?

Because to finish the race well, the fuel of favor will be required. This year I'm praying for favor for your life and for the real love movement called Faith Promise Church.

Can you imagine what would happen if every Promisor saw an increase of favor and blessing on their life, family, and ministry? I'm praying favor is a mark on each Promisor.

At the end of each day is a Faith Declaration. If you've been a part of Faith Promise for long, you may have seen these in previous devotionals.

Let me ask you to take the Faith Declarations seriously. Speaking words of life out loud straight from Scripture will increase your faith and you will see God's favor at work moving forward.

Faith **"calls into being that which does not exist." – Romans 4:17**

This daily discipline comes from the Greek word *homologia* or "say the same word." Sometimes I am shocked to hear the words which proceed from the mouths of other followers of Christ.

Like the early Israelites, too many confess sour outlooks, bitter circumstances, and little hope for the future. Too few speak favor and faith into situations. Please spend the end of each day letting expectations of favor flow from your mouth.

Do you believe God desires to pour out His favor on you? I do.

So, let me challenge you to actually say each Faith Declaration out loud. Say it with passion and faith, believing your declaration.

God said, **"Death and life are in the power of the tongue."** **– Proverbs 18:21**

God spoke, and **the universe was created. – Genesis 1:3**

He also said, **"It shall be done to you according to your faith." – Matthew 9:29**

I could list more passages, but instead, let's look forward to a month that will change your life. I'm grateful for your taking the time to experience Him for the next 31 days. I pray Godly habits will form and that you will begin to see God's favor at work more than ever before.

No matter what happened last year. No matter what happens this year. No matter what—after this month in *Finding Favor*—you will see God's favor at work.

Six Ways to Fast

What is a fast?

A fast is typically when you give up certain foods and drinks, or give up all food and drink entirely, for some amount of time.

Why should I consider fasting?

1. To strengthen your prayer (Ezra 8:23)
2. To seek God's wisdom (1 Samuel 31:13)
3. To humble ourselves before God (1 Kings 21:27-30)
4. To worship God (Luke 2:37)

What are some common kinds of fasts?

Daniel Fast (Daniel 10:3)

Daniel fasted for 21 days and gave up "delicacies" like meat and wine.

One Meal Fast

Fast one meal a day and instead devote the time normally spent eating to prayer.

Technology/Media Fast

Fast all or some technology or media and instead devote the time normally spent engaging this technology or media to prayer.

When is the 2021 Faith Promise Churchwide fast?

The fast will begin on Monday, January 4, 2021 and end on Sunday, January 24, 2021.

What will I fast:

_____

_____

_____

When will I devote time to prayer:

_____

_____

_____

Who/what will I pray for during this fast:

_____

_____

_____

— Day One —
THE SOURCE

"Let the favor of the Lord our God be upon us; And confirm for us the work of our hands; Yes, confirm the work of our hands."
– Psalm 90:17

Daily Devotion

Just in case you're someone who does not read introductions or you only skimmed the pages before today, Psalm 90:17 is our theme verse for the year! And what an incredible year is ahead of us. I believe 2021 is going to be the greatest year in the history of our church.

I love this verse in Psalm 90 and pray it over our church all the time. In it, the psalmist writes a bold prayer, asking for the favor of God. He goes to God because He is the source. Two times the writer asks for God's favor to be on the work of his hands.

Almost every day, I ask for the same thing. In 2020, my word was "Favor." After a year of praying and studying favor, I believe that God's favor is already at work in the life of every believer. The question is, will we see it and walk in it? Favor is a mark on our lives and far more than just positive thinking.

Sadly, too many people look for favor from other fountains. Some seek favor from relationships, family, careers, or the government. However, those fountains are bone dry. All of God's favor and blessings flow from Him because God alone is the source and Living Water.

When we read the Old Testament, the Hebrew people often addressed God by different names. One of the names is Jehovah-Jireh, which means "God is the Provider." As Christians, we must recognize God as the source.

You might ask, "Pastor, what does it mean to recognize God as the source?"

It means acknowledging God alone sits on the throne of our hearts. God is our greatest Treasure, our first Priority, our King, our Judge, and our good Father. And although God is the source of all favor, here is the key...

We are to go after *God*, not His blessings!
We follow the Father and not just His favor.

This month, we will practice walking with Him daily and seeking out His favor. The Bible is full of verses about the favor of God on His people. I believe when we seek the heart and face of God, we will find His favor and be comforted by it like a warm blanket on a cold night.

You can trust God and His Word. I have watched His favor pour out on me and my family more and more each year. I never dreamed I would be here and get to see and do all I get to see and do. I live in awe of His overflowing favor.

Now, if you're thinking "all this favor stuff sounds great for you, Pastor, but it's not for me. You don't understand my circumstances or situation." Let me encourage you with this truth: there is always hope with a limitless supernatural God.

This year *will* be your year. You *will* get healthy. You *will* lose weight. You *will* graduate. You *will* become debt-free. You *will* overcome your addiction. God's favor is a force to take you where He wants you to go.

Whatever mountain is blocking your way, God can move it. Whatever your disease, God can heal it. Whatever you are facing is not bigger than God. God is your source and a bottomless well of blessings and favor that will never run dry.

Faith Declaration

God is my source. He provides everything I need and more. This year I will see God's favor and walk in it. By faith, I believe this will be my best year ever.

Question and Response

Every year at Faith Promise, we encourage our church to seek out a word and corresponding verse from Scripture for the year. What is your word and verse for 2021? (See the next page.)

What could success look like for your word?

Praise	Friend	Unbind	Celebra
Rely	Companion	Teeming	Delight
Favor	Leader	Proud	Courag
Faith	Zealous	Change	Humility
Perseverance	Embrace	Joy	Resist
Listen	Overcome	Try	Renew
Purpose	Breathe	Commit	Decisior
Create	Focus		Accept
Diligent	E		memb.
Wait			nStar
Praise			ebra
Rely			ight
Favor			Courag
Faith	Zealous	Change	Humility
Perseverance	Embrace	Joy	Resist
Listen	Overcome	Try	Renew
Purpose	Breathe	Commit	Decisior
Create	Focus	Laugh	Accept
Diligent	Efficient	Teach	Rememb
Wait	Honest	Learn	Withsta
Praise	Friend	Unbind	Celebra
Rely	Companion	Teeming	Deligh
Favor	Leader	Proud	Courag

Write your word of the year on the rock below.

Prayers answered

Grateful for

How did God move?

—— Day Two ——
PERSPECTIVE

"Draw near to God, and He will draw near to you."
– James 4:8

Daily Devotion

The number one value at Faith Promise is *We Put God First.* When you put God first, God commands His favor to be in and on your life. Does that mean you will not experience pain or problems? Absolutely not! In fact, your pain and problems could even increase!

Still, part of believing and receiving God's commanded favor is keeping a cosmic Christ perspective. Too many of us are tempted to focus on our circumstances and not on Christ.

Let's be real! Do we wake up every morning and reflect on Jesus' death on the cross? Do we get cut off on the interstate and think about the blood Jesus shed for our sins? Do we open a past due bill and think about the New Heavens and New Earth in our future? Of course not! We are caught up in our pain and problems.

But God is bigger than your circumstances!

No matter what the doctor, your boss, or even your friends and family members say, God's commanded favor can overcome anything and everything. God said, "Let there be light," and it happened.

When the Creator of the entire cosmos commands favor, the forces of hell cannot stop it. God can pour out when everyone and everything else is dry. He can put you in the right places, rain down incredible opportunities, and move you forward when no one else expects it.

But Pastor, I never catch a break. All I have is bad luck. Stop! Do not believe those lies about your life. God gets the last word! He has all power and authority, not the people and circumstances in your life.

Look up and see how God is at work!

In Numbers 22, the Hebrew people were newly released slaves, leaving Egypt en route to Jericho and the Promised Land. King Balak of the Moabites sees how mighty the army of Israel is, and knows he can't defeat them. So, he hires a prophet named Balaam to curse Israel. The hired prophet Balaam sees Israel but does not curse them. Instead, he blesses them! King Balak is furious, but the prophet replies,

> **"Behold, I have received a command to bless;**
> **When He has blessed, then I cannot revoke it."**
> **– Numbers 23:20**

Nothing can stop the commanded blessings and favor of God from being poured out on you. Regardless of your current circumstances, God commands His favor. He can heal. He can restore. He can replace. Favor is God's force to carry you to His desired destiny for you.

So, let's change our perspective and look up to see how God's favor is already at work! Don't skip this next part— actually take a minute to boldly declare out loud today's Faith Declaration.

Faith Declaration

Today, I will put God first. I will focus on the power of the
Father, the mighty name of Jesus, and the comforting peace
of the Holy Spirit. No matter what, I will see God's favor at
work in my life today.

Question + Response

Take a few minutes to reflect on your life today. Where do
you see the blessing and favor of God in your life? What
circumstances are blocking your view of our limitless God?

Prayers answered

Grateful for

How did God move?

GIFTS

"If you then, being evil, know how to give good gifts to your children,
how much more will your Father who is in heaven
give what is good to those who ask Him!"
– Matthew 7:11

Daily Devotion

What comes to mind when you think of God? Do you see
God as distant and too far away to care about your everyday
struggles? Do you see God as always angry and ready to
bring the holy hammer down every time you slip up? Or
do you think of God like a fire truck, only there in times of
emergency?

A great Christian pastor, A.W. Tozer, once wrote, "What
comes into our minds when we think about God is the most
important thing about us." The crazy thing is, we can miss
out on all the favor the Lord planned for us just because we
hold a wrong view of God. If you missed yesterday, go back
and check out what I mean.

Jesus offers us an illustration of the Father's favor, reminding
us, **"If you being evil, know how to give good gifts to your
children, how much more will My Father give to those who
ask."**

God gives every good gift! He loves to bless His kids more
than the best parent you know wants to bless their children.
When you bend your knee to King Jesus, God adopts you
into His family. Think about it. The God of the universe is
now your adopted Father. And I believe God looks for ways
to bless you and pour out His favor on you!

However, if we are not careful, our view of God can change. Instead of seeing a generous Father giving amazing gifts, we can think of God as absent, indifferent to our circumstances, or worse, maybe even cruel and unkind on purpose. These wrong views can lead us to swimming against the current, struggling to get ahead, and missing God's favor at work.

And when we begin to expect bad things to happen or look forward to poor results, we begin to have a poor view of God and often end up getting exactly what we expected.

Jaclyn and Phil's Story

One weekend during a time of worship, Phil and I saw the same vision from God. This vision was of us living in and loving the people in Lenoir City in a home that was an open place for ministry.

There was only one problem. We lived miles away in a budget-friendly ranch house which we bought early in our marriage and were almost done paying off.

In the natural, we were scared to sell and move. But we believed God was working, so we followed the Spirit's lead. Then, our house sold fast and our wandering began.

Often, we felt like the Israelites following God's pillar of fire in the dark of night, as we struggled to find a home in our price range which fit God's vision for this work He was going to do through us.

We believed His vision required a basement for people needing temporary housing and an open floor plan for hosting large groups and friends. We were not looking for a fancy house, just a *shalom* one—a place where those in need could experience peace.

After months of searching and renting, offers and counteroffers, bank calls and stressful nights, tears and tough decisions, God guided us to an incredible two-story house with an unfinished basement.

Seven years later we finished the basement, and so far, have provided temporary housing for several people in need. We host Fusion and Movement students every year. We host a group and our group has multiplied several times!

This home is not only a blessing to us and a real example of God's favor, but we believe is and continues to be a gift to all who enter its' doors.

God's blessings and favor are at work all around us, but if we allow comparison to cloud our vision, we can miss those gifts and be left empty and wanting more. What gift from God are you thankful for today?

Jaclyn Holloway and her husband, Phil, have served Faith Promise for more than 10 years. She currently serves on staff as the fpCreative Project Manager.

Faith Declaration

Today is a gift from God! Today will be an incredible day! I choose joy. I choose to celebrate. My Heavenly Father loves to bless His kids, and I believe He will pour out His favor on me.

Question + Response

When Jesus looks at you, what do you believe He thinks?
(Hint: John 15:15, Ephesians 2:10, Deuteronomy 7:6, and 2
Corinthians 6:18)

_____

_____

_____

_____

Now, describe how you view God in four or five words.

_____

_____

_____

_____

Prayers answered

Grateful for

How did God move?

— Day Four —
MOUNTAINS

"Consecrate a fast, proclaim a solemn assembly;
Gather the elders and all the inhabitants of the land
to the house of the Lord your God, and cry out to the Lord."
– Joel 1:14

Daily Devotion

One of my favorite verses in the Hebrew Scriptures comes from the prophet Zechariah. God gives Zechariah a word of wisdom to share with Zerubbabel, the governor.

"'Not by might nor by power, but by My Spirit,' says the Lord of hosts."
– Zechariah 4:6

Western culture ingrains in us the belief that success comes from power and effort. We pull ourselves up by our bootstraps. We get it done. But God says, "[...] By My power, you succeed."

We miss so much when we focus on our abilities and not His. Our God is without equal and nothing compares to Him. However, instead of looking up to focus on Him and His works, we try and solve our problems with our works.

Zechariah tells Zerubbabel, "Go and speak to the mountain."

For Zerubbabel and Zechariah, the mountain represented their insurmountable difficulties. The mountain was an overwhelming sense of discouragement experienced by the displaced Hebrew people. Zerubbabel wanted to rebuild God's temple, but everything seemed stacked against him.

So, Zechariah told the governor to speak to his problems and to speak to his challenges, because something happens when we speak out loud against these challenges. Something happens when we speak out God's favor and declare what He can do.

This is why the daily Faith Declarations in our devotionals are such important moments for you to proclaim God's favor. I practice daily Faith Declarations in my prayer journal, and since I began sharing what I write, Promisors come up to me all the time asking me to write statements for them.

In this devotional, I wrote 31 moments just for you. Borrow them and then create your own Faith Declarations. Speak to your mountains and declare the blessings and favor of God!

If we look at problems and don't see a way out, don't see miracles, don't see weight loss, debt paid off, disease healed, or job offers coming—if we look down and mutter to ourselves, "I have tried before. What's the point?"—we will not see God's favor at work.

Let me challenge you to look up and see how God's already at work. Yes, right now. Now, this time try with God's power! Try with God's favor! God is not stingy! He is not limited in His power or His miracles! Jesus said,

> **"Ask, and you will receive, seek, and you will find, knock, and it will be opened to you." – Matthew 7:7**

By the way, Zerubbabel was able to finish the impossible project of the Temple reconstruction. How? Not by his own might and power, but through God's Spirit and favor at work. God has big plans for you. Are you ready?

Faith Declaration

I will walk by the power and Spirit of God. I rely on Your ability, God, not my own. I may start small, but God will do something big. God will give me insight during this fast. He will give me revelation.

Question + Response

First day of Fast: How will you seek God during the next 21 days?

_____

_____

_____

_____

Where are you asking God to move in your life and how will He cover you with favor?

_____

_____

_____

_____

Overcoming Your Mountain

What Mountains Are You Overcoming?

(Write them in the space below)

Prayers answered

Grateful for

How did God move?

—— Day Five ——
WORDS

"The words of a man's mouth are deep waters;
The fountain of wisdom is a bubbling brook."
– Proverbs 18:4

Daily Devotion

Every word coming out of your mouth is powerful. Few of us consider the weight of our words. Jesus' brother, James, gives great insight into the power of the tongue.

Take a quick moment and read James 3:1-6.

Like a rudder turning a large ship, can you see how something as small as the tongue can turn around a difficult situation you're facing?

Like a small flame destroys a forest, can you see how something as small as your tongue can transform a gift from God into nothing more than ash?

When we speak, we release something into the atmosphere and hearts of everyone listening. Our words can change the course of a life and ignite faith. Every day I speak to God's favor at work and believe God for increase in Faith Promise and in my own life. Many Promisors believe in God's favor, and yet so few of us dare to speak it!

See and speak to God's favor at work over your family, group, ministry, health, and finances.

Jesus said in Matthew 12:36, "But I tell you that every careless word that people speak, they shall give an accounting for it in the day of judgment."

When we experience real pain and problems or tough circumstances—and let's be real, we all will—it does not mean God has abandoned us. It may be an opportunity to see God's favor at work like never before.

So, the next time troubles come, speak favor and life not fear and death. How many times have you said,

"I will never make it."
"I always get sick."
"Nothing good ever happens to me."
"I never get any breaks."

In Jesus' name, stop speaking death! If you truly want to start finding favor, start speaking life and victory and favor over yourself and others.

In Paul's letter to the church in Rome, he writes of how Jesus sits at the right hand of the Father and intercedes for us. (**Romans 8:34**) Now, just imagine for a second the Triune God in an emergency meeting looking for and seeking out new ways to bless you.

How about what David wrote in Psalm 23:6, "Surely goodness and loving kindness will follow me all the days of my life." The two words loving and kindness actually represent one word in Hebrew, *hesed*.

Hesed is the kindness, love, and favor God shows His people. Think of it like this, favor is a blessing chasing you down. And here's the good news, you can no more outrun God's favor than you can outrun God.

Robbie's Story

Every Sunday, a group gathers in Pastor Chris' office at the Pellissippi Campus. It is not anything fancy. There is no breakfast or music. Just eight or nine people sitting in chairs. Men and women who show up early every week to knock on the door of heaven and cover all of our campuses in prayer. Each person takes a few minutes to pray for the message, to pray for the people hearing the message, and to ask for the Holy Spirit to move in power.

One Sunday four or five years ago, someone spoke some sticky words over my life. You know what I mean by sticky words, right? Remember the old school rhyme, "I am rubber, you are glue. Whatever I say bounces off me and sticks to you." Some words stick to us.

After I finished praying, Pastor Chris reached out his hand and placed it on my shoulder. "God, thank You for calling Robbie to be a leader. Today he is a leader of tens and hundreds. But I know that You are calling him to be a leader of thousands. A leader of tens of thousands."

It took me a few minutes to process those words. "Wow, a leader of tens of thousands."

Those words activated something. A few years have gone by since Pastor Chris prayed those words and this prodigal son is now a prodigal pastor. And ever since that morning years ago, every time I face a challenge in leadership, those sticky words flood and fill my heart and mind.

I still believe those words. I can do this. I can do the great things God has called me to do. I am a leader of thousands. A leader of tens of thousands.

The words you speak to others can bring life and overflowing favor.

Robbie Freeman is our Groups and Missions Pastor at the North Knox Campus. He sat with me in Pastor's Prayer Partners for four years before God called him to ministry.

Now Promisors, before you go out and see God's favor at work today, speak today's Faith Declaration out loud and in faith!

Faith Declaration

I will speak life today. I will speak life to myself and to everyone I encounter. Today God will use my mouth to produce fresh living water. I will be an encourager and my words, through the power of the Holy Spirit, will bring life. The power of life and death is in my mouth and I will choose life.

Question + Response

The Bible is one of the best ways for us to understand the mind of God and is our Word of Life. What is your plan for reading the Bible this year? (Example: check out Faith Promise's Bible Reading Plan at faithpromise.org)

_____

_____

_____

Challenge: Start your day by texting someone words of life.

Prayers answered

Grateful for

How did God move?

—— Day Six ——
CONNECTIONS

" Iron sharpens iron,
So one man sharpens another."
– Proverbs 27:17

Daily Devotion

Do you really want the favor of God in your life?

Think back to the beginning of the week. What was our first step? To Put God First, because God is the source. We must seek Him, not His favor. And when we go looking for all of God, all of His favor finds us.

So, what is one of the easiest ways to go looking for more of God?

"Now you are Christ's body, and individually members of it.
And God has appointed in the church, first apostles, second prophets,
third teachers, then miracles, then gifts of healings, helps,
administrations, various kinds of tongues."
– 1 Corinthians 12:27-28

The Church is the body of Christ and one of the most vital ways of connecting with God's favor. There is an enormous amount of favor flowing from this local movement of Christ called Faith Promise. Do you see it?

Last year we talked about the connection to the Church and I challenged every Promisor to go ALL iN. Like a network of pipes, the Church is connected to the Source of favor, the Triune God. When we worship, grow, serve, and give together, favor flows in us and through us to everyone around us!

Together, we can find favor!

However, while some connections help us see more of God's favor at work, others can block our view and hinder favor from flowing. In my life, several incredible people who have been conduits of God's favor are my pastor, Chris Hodges, from Church of the Highlands, Coach Tom Mullins, and my leadership mentor, John Maxwell. Each of them challenges me to grow and helps me see and experience the favor of God daily.

Who in your life is helping you see and experience increased blessings and favor?

In 1 Kings 19, when the prophet Elijah called the farmer Elisha to follow him, Elisha was not a leader. But as the favor flowed down, Elisha ended up with the same double anointing as his mentor, Elijah. When we connect with Spirit-filled and favored leaders, God's favor drips down all over us. I believe the Lord puts people in your path to help you. Ask God for the wisdom and discernment to see those people.

"But Pastor, I'm not connected to anyone with favor."

No problem, let me help you! One of our values at Faith Promise is *We Grow Together*. You see, God provides people and relationships in our lives to be fountains of favor. As the book of Proverbs says, **"As iron sharpens iron, so one person sharpens another." (Proverbs 27:17)** The best way to experience a sharpening is to grind your way into a group!

Once God's favor is on your life, it can begin to flow to others around you.

In the book of Genesis is an example of one of the most favored people in the whole Old Testament: Jacob. God changed his name to Israel, and his twelve sons multiplied into the nation of Israel. When Jacob was young, he set his eyes on a pretty lady named Rachel. However, to win his bride, Rachel's father-in-law put him to work. Later, Jacob does so well farming that his father-in-law tries to force Jacob to stay longer. Laban tells him, **"If now it pleases you, stay with me; I have divined that the Lord has blessed me on your account."** Laban saw the favor increase in his life and livelihood from the mere presence of his son-in-law. Laban knew his additional blessing was because of Jacob.

There are many ways to go looking for God and find His favor at work. The only question is, are you connected to any of them?

Faith Declaration

I will be humble and teachable. I will be ready to learn from anyone who will help me find favor. I will be alert and see the relationships God puts in my path. God will open up critical connections to help me see God's favor at work.

Question + Response

In the jerseys on the next page, write the names of the people who fulfill these positions in your life.

In the jerseys below, write the names of people who fulfill these positions in your life.

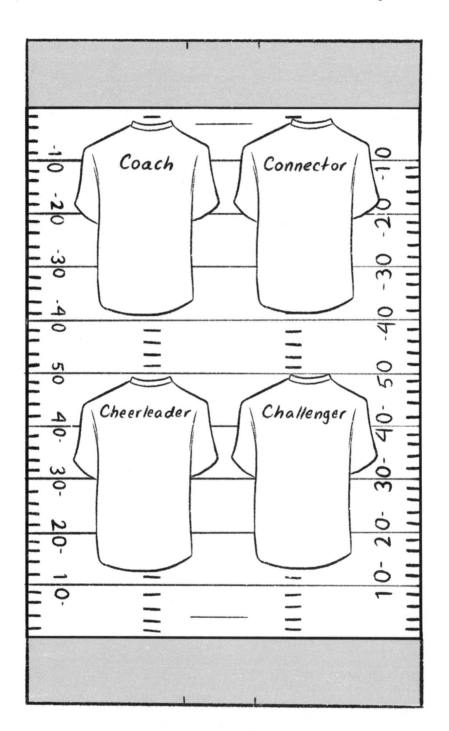

Prayers answered

Grateful for

How did God move?

OPEN DOORS

> "And I will make you a great nation,
> And I will bless you,
> And make your name great;
> And so you shall be a blessing."
> – Genesis 12:2

Daily Devotion

As we saw yesterday, who we connect to and surround ourselves with can affect our view and access to the flow of God's favor already at work in our lives. I truly believe you are one connection, one prayer, and one introduction away from incredible opportunities.

Maybe you think it will never happen for you. Maybe the thought of meeting new people makes you queasy. Maybe you do not believe you can find those kind of connections. But, here's the truth:

New favor requires new faith.

Before becoming the greatest King in Israel, David was a nobody. Jesse, David's dad, kept him busy in the back pasture taking care of the sheep. And when God sent the prophet Samuel to Jesse's door to anoint the next King of Israel, Jesse paraded each of his sons in front of the man of God—each son except for his youngest, David.

While sending his taller, smarter, and stronger sons forward to receive Samuel's blessing, it somehow never seems to occur to Jesse to call David in from herding sheep.

Have you ever felt forgotten in the back or left out alone in the pasture?

Jesse must have thought God would pick the ones with the most potential in the eyes of the world. But God's favor is available and at work for everyone, even those forgotten and seemingly left out.

Before Samuel left, the prophet asks Jesse, "Do you have any other sons?" Confused, Jesse replies, "Yes, but just little 'ol David, who is out watching the sheep. It can't be him." But as soon as David walked in, God spoke to Samuel, and said, "Yes! He is the one." (**1 Samuel 16:12**)

Can you imagine the shock in that moment?

Only God holds your destiny. I believe today you are one relationship and one connection from seeing His favored future for you. If that doesn't feel true right now, think about the morning for David when Samuel came to visit. David woke up, got dressed, and went out to watch the sheep like every other morning.

David didn't know Samuel was coming *that* day. David couldn't even dream that God was about to unlock his destiny! I pray as you seek out God today He reveals His favor. And more importantly, that you say yes! I pray you have faith to see His favor and seize it.

King David became a great warrior and leader of God, but not without a connection to someone with favor who helped unlock the door to his destiny. In the name of Jesus, dare to dream today of a greater future with greater favor and an influx of influence!

Rob's Story

It's the bottom of the ninth, bases loaded, two outs, and a rookie steps up to the plate for his first major league at bat. You know the rest of the story, right? He hits a home run and is the hero of the game. This was my childhood dream.

But, when I was about five years old, my mom shared a different dream with me. In a story she retold many times, Mom said, "When you were born, I gave you to God for His purposes." And as I grew older, she would say, "Rob, one day you will be a pastor."

Constantly, she reminded me of her agreement with God on the day I was born. And I would reply, "No way." Or "Come on mom. Enough with the pastor stuff." But I must admit, a little piece of her dream stayed with me.

In 1984 while living and working in Kansas City, home of my favorite baseball team, the Royals, my company's season tickets kept giving me countless opportunities to enjoy a lot of home games. And I was actually there when the Royals won their first World Series in 1985.

Sitting in those stands, I remember thinking, "I am living the dream."

Little did I know 30 years later I would end up living a whole new dream. A dream even better than my own. A dream my mother shared with me so many years ago.

No, I never ended up playing professional baseball and I left the city where I spent so many afternoons watching my favorite team play. And sure, at one point in my life, I thought my dream was baseball, making money, and succeeding in business, but I have to admit—Mom knew better.

I may never hit a game-winning home run and cross home plate to thunderous applause, but I do get to help people find their way home in groups. And instead of cheering the Royals from the stands, I am on the field helping people round the bases and take the next step in their relationship with God.

Now, when people ask what it is like being a pastor at Faith Promise, I get to tell them for real, "I am living the dream."

Rob Patrick is a leader of leaders and worked in the engineering, testing, and exploration industry for years before God called him out. Now, Rob is the Pastor of Groups and Missions at the Pellissippi Campus.

Faith Declaration

Today, God will open doors no one can close. I am one connection away from seeing God's increasing favor at work and moving toward the destiny God planned for me. I will move forward on full alert for His mighty works.

Question + Response

Who in your life helps you see and connect with God's favor?

_____

_____

_____

_____

What big decisions will you make to change the quality of your relationship with God and with those important to you?

_____

_____

_____

_____

Prayers answered

Grateful for

How did God move?

—— Day Eight ——
SIGNET RING

"'On that day,' declares the LORD of hosts, 'I will take you, Zerubbabel, son of Shealtiel, My servant,' declares the LORD, 'and I will make you like a signet ring, for I have chosen you,' declares the LORD of hosts."
– Haggai 2:23

Daily Devotion

The favor of God sets us apart. God's favor is a stamp, a seal, a mark. Even people far from God can recognize favor when they see it at work in the King's kids.

In Exodus 33, God singles Moses out by name to receive His favor. But, as usual, this was not enough for Moses. He wanted the signet ring kind of favor. The favor that seals. So, he prays to God and declares, "Then he said to Him, "If Your presence does not go *with us*, do not lead us up from here." – Exodus 33:15

God's glory and His favor prove our adoption by God.

Now remember, God's favor does not exclude real pain and problems or trials and tribulations, and struggles are not a sign of God's favor fading. Quite the opposite. The favor of God is always working and carries us through tough circumstances. Even while wandering in the wilderness, Israel walked under the glory of God. And we can experience His favor in trials because He is present with us in the fire (Daniel 3).

When Joseph's older brothers sold him into slavery because of his dream that they would bow to him like a king, they never imagined his dream would come true. What his brothers meant for evil, God meant for good!

Only God holds our destiny in His Hand. Only God's favor gives us what we need when trials come. Despite setback after setback on Joseph's terrible journey, God eventually exalted him. Even people far from God saw the favor of the Lord in Joseph's life.

Once upon a time, kings and monarchs wore signet rings as a sign of their power, and signet rings were used like stamps to seal contracts, letters, and commands issued by the ruler or authority.

Promisors, we are ambassadors and representatives of God's Kingdom and His favor is our signet ring. Once He stamps us with the favor of the Lord, we are wearing His endorsement and official stamp of approval for all the world to see.

God's favor at work sustained Zerubbabel and that same favor at work will support you. Raise your head. You are not defeated! Look up and see His favor working! We must always worship and serve the Lord in even the direst circumstances so everyone will see how great is our God.

Enemies and difficulties may come against you, but you will remain stable because you have the signet ring and God's favor on you. Slip the favor of the Lord on your finger today and walk in His limitless favor as He pours it out. Receive every ounce of it to see your designed destiny develop.

Faith Declaration

I am chosen. Today God's favor is at work in my life and I
will wear His favor as a signet ring. His favor sets me apart
and even people far from God will recognize His favor on
me.

Question + Response

Think of someone's testimony that has impacted you. What
was it about their story that glorified Jesus and revealed
God's favor at work?

What is preventing you from being a shiny ring showing
God's favor? Attitude, insecurity, pride, sin?

Prayers answered

Grateful for

How did God move?

COSMIC TRIALS

"Sanctify Christ as Lord in your hearts, always being ready to make a
defense to everyone who asks you to give an account for the hope that is
in you, yet with gentleness and reverence."
– 1 Peter 3:15

Daily Devotion

Let me be raw and real for a minute. Sometimes it is hard to
see God's favor and believe for blessings when facing cosmic
circumstances. Don't you agree?

As I write this, the COVID-19 pandemic spreads across the
world. We cannot buy toilet paper or cleaning supplies at
the store. Even more challenging, Faith Promise has not met
in a building for three months, and for the first time in our
history, we prepared and executed our first ever Easter only
online!

Many Promisors lost their jobs or were furloughed. Some
who were on the verge of retirement lost small fortunes
in their 401Ks. Every day the news reports more cases of
coronavirus, more deaths, more destruction, all from an
invisible enemy. All across the world, people feel as though
they have lost control. Fear, anxiety, suicide, and depression
are rampant. These circumstances are cosmic.

Think back to 2020. What do you remember? Do you
remember the injustice, protests, riots, and division? Do you
see the potential or only the problems?

When we focus on the problems, we can easily be discouraged or distracted from our destiny. And if we let those problems overwhelm us, the defeat can become our identity. But, if you are a Christ follower, your identity is not found in your circumstances. Your identity is found in Christ.

In truth, during difficult times is when favor shines the brightest. When you look and live above and beyond the circumstances instead of being dragged down by them, your outlook and favor will set you apart from everyone around you.

Your calmness in the storm will cause people to ask about the Hope that is in you.

A believer I know who walks in favor despite cosmic circumstances is my friend, Pastor Josh Whitehead. As many of you know, his wife, Kim, passed away this fall after an incredibly long and courageous battle against cancer. And although her eternal victory and healing is a clear example of God's favor, it's hard to see how her absence on earth could possibly be described as God's favor to the family and friends she leaves on this side of eternity.

This may surprise you, but I cannot think of someone I know personally who better illustrates God's favor more than Josh. He lived in, and sometimes still visits, a place the psalmist calls the "valley of the shadow of death." And yet, even today, he walks with an unwavering belief in the goodness of God. He works with and gives the Lord his best efforts and he pushes every day to expand God's kingdom. He prays for others with a smile on his face. There will still be difficult days and moments ahead, but I know with certainty Josh will continue to care for his children, Hayden and Madison, and for any others who need the real love of Jesus, to the utmost of his ability.

If I'm being real, I'm not sure I could do what Josh has done. Despite the worst circumstances, he walked faithfully in his marital vows, fatherhood, and ministry. When I see his kids thriving, serving, and blessing the people of Faith Promise with gladness, I cannot think of a better example of walking in and walking out God's favor.

The Whitehead family is a beacon of God's favor and a living testimony of real faith. They walk in joy at church, at school, and at home. Talk about surrender. What if we all surrendered to the Source like Josh did in the valley of the shadow of death? What could God pour out in our lives and in the lives of our families?

Faith Declaration

I have God's favor. I will look and live above and beyond circumstances and refuse to be dragged down by the enemy's efforts. God's Hand is on me and He will care for me even in the valley of the shadow of death. I will focus on God and His Word alone.

Question + Response

Write down what comes to mind when you
think back to 2020.

_____

_____

_____

_____

What did God teach you during the time of
COVID-19?

_____

_____

_____

_____

Prayers answered

Grateful for

How did God move?

OUT OF THE BLUE

> "And coming in, he said to her,
> 'Greetings, favored one! The Lord is with you.'"
> – Luke 1:28

Daily Devotion

Most of us look at ourselves as normal, average, followers of Christ. We just get by in life and drift day-to-day like we aren't *really* recipients of God's favor. How easy is it believe that God only uses talented people or gifted people?

Do you find it easy to think, "What's so special about me, anyway?" Perhaps you cannot even imagine what God's favor flowing over you would even look like or feel like this year. Be real, is that you? It's okay, that's honestly most of us. Here's the truth:

God really does use real people with real problems to advance His Kingdom.

Read Hebrews 11 and look at the list of the Hall of Fame of faith. All of those names were ordinary people just like us. Then one day, the fountain of favor began to flow and everything changed!

Mary, the mother of Jesus, is one of those ordinary people who experienced the fountain of favor. Mary was just a poor young woman anxiously looking forward to her wedding with Joseph. Then one day, some two thousand years ago, an angel appears and says, **"Greetings, favored one, the Lord is with you." – Luke 1:28**

The Bible says Mary was "perplexed," which in the Pastor Chris edition is translated from Greek as "freaking out!" Who wouldn't be freaked out by this sudden angelic appearance?!

Do you think Mary thought of herself as "the favored one?" Probably not, but God did! And it is the same for us. Many of us wouldn't describe ourselves as favored, blessed, or the apple of God's eye. Many of us don't see ourselves this way so we don't expect supernatural favor to flow in us and through us. But, know this, Promisor—God delights in you!

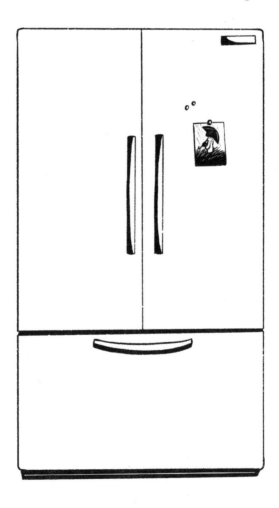

Take a moment and talk to God about how you are His favored one. Don't talk yourself out of it. Thank the Lord Mary didn't talk herself out of it. While she was pregnant, she visited the home of her aunt, who was pregnant with John the Baptist.

Elizabeth told Mary, **"Blessed is she who believed [...] what had been spoken to her by the Lord."** (Luke 1:45). Remember, Mary was just a poor young fiancée until she believed what the Lord said. Now, two thousand years later, we still talk about her. Talk about blessing the works of our hands! Mary's body carried Jesus, the Lord and the Author of our salvation.

Mary is a hero of faith! Not because she was great, but because she believed for great favor. Do you? Mary's life changed overnight. I wonder what God might do for you or through you today.

Brittany's Story

Last year during our 21 Days of Prayer and Fasting, I felt divinely connected to God. I was looking ahead to what I hoped would be my first days of parenting. During the last week of our fast, I sensed God saying that my first foster placement would come. And around 10:00 p.m. on November 5, Sophia and Alyssa arrived at my doorstep.

I opened the door and heard the heartbreaking cries of five broken children, three of whom were going to a different home. As I stepped onto the porch that night, I stepped into the footprints of God's wisdom and discernment and looked at Alyssa, and in my black momma voice told her, "Hug me."

After putting the girls to bed, I clearly could hear God saying, "Leave your door open." And later that night, Alyssa came into my room and we talked and talked in a wonderful conversation about Jesus and faith.

A few days later, I got a call. Alyssa was going to be released to her father. Confused and unsure of what to do next, I went to God for wisdom. He comforted me with flashbacks of our first night together.

The memory was perfect. Some people might just call it a coincidence, but I know it was His favor. I know it was God working out of the blue.

Brittany Pollard is an amazing woman of God who moved here from California to serve as an fpKIDS Pastor at the Pellissippi Campus. Brittany's heart for the next generation is lived out on the front lines by bringing God's favor to her kids as a foster parent.

Faith Declaration

God, you will use me any way you see fit today. You will put me wherever You choose. God, I believe You will give me greater gifts, ministry, and miracles. Today, I will look for an "out of the blue" mighty move of God.

Question + Response

When God unleashes His incredible favor out of the blue, how will you respond?

Prayers answered

Grateful for

How did God move?

SET APART

"You were bought with a price; do not become slaves of men."
– 1 Corinthians 7:23

Daily Devotion

Do you believe followers of Jesus should be different than people far from God? How so? What sets us apart? Our words, our actions, our attitudes, our priorities? Sure. Do you know what else sets us apart? God's favor.

The Holy Spirit inspired Peter to write this about you. "You are a chosen race, a royal priesthood, a holy nation, a people for God's own possession." (**1 Peter 2:9**). As Christ followers, he says we will act, look, and live differently.

We are anointed, appointed, and set apart.

The way we live is different and part of the light Jesus calls us to shine. People should see our freedom, faith, forgiveness, and favor and want what we have.

Look at how the favor of God protected and prospered the Israelites in the book of Exodus. The Egyptians saw something different in the Israelites than they saw in themselves. Before Moses arrived on the scene, the Egyptians looked on the Hebrew people with disdain. The Egyptians viewed themselves as superior, and believed the Jews only existed to serve them. However, when God's favor arrived with Moses and Aaron, the story shifts. Ten plagues fall on the Egyptians, while each time the Jewish people are spared.

No plagues, no problems, and no judgment.

The Egyptians still see the Israelites as different, but now they envy them. Pharaoh releases the Jews from slavery, and the citizens of Egypt give their former slaves gold, silver, and money. What changed? Now, the favor of God was evident in Goshen, the area where the Israelites lived. Egypt saw the favor of God on Israel.

Still, despite all this, there were times when the Israelites forgot about this great favor. In the wilderness, they begged Moses to send them back to Egypt. They didn't see themselves free and highly favored, instead they saw themselves as slaves, despising the desert. They did not see God's favor at work.

Does this sound familiar?

In the wilderness, God and His servant, Moses, repeatedly tried to drive out this slave mentality, but with little lasting success. What about you? Do you also see yourself through this lens? Constant negative words and outlook signify a slave mentality. Just like the children of Israel, we were born into slavery—slavery to sin. However, when you give your heart to Jesus, you are forgiven and freed. If you are born again, you are adopted by God.

You are no longer a slave to sin! As a matter of theological fact, God forgets your sin. Israel never earned their way out of slavery, it was reckoned to them through God's grace. We don't earn our freedom either. God's grace gives us mercy. By His mercy, we are free!

God handpicked you! He chose you to love you and pour His favor on you. He decided to bless you with life instead of cursing you with death because of His Son's great work on a Roman cross.

God's favor at work is a reminder of your freedom and that you are set apart.

Faith Declaration

I am set apart! I will walk in God's love, acceptance, and forgiveness as a child of God. I was bought with a price and I will shine His light and pour out His favor on everyone I meet today.

Question + Response

What does each of these Bible verses say about your identity in Jesus?

1 John 3:1 | I am_____

1 Peter 2:9 | I am _____

John 15:15 | I am _____

Philippians 3:20 | I am _____

Prayers answered

Grateful for

How did God move?

GLORIFY GOD

"And they were glorifying God because of me."
– Galatians 1:24

Daily Devotion

The apostle Paul was a radical follower of Jesus. I love what he wrote in Galatians. "I was still unknown by sight to the churches of Judea which were in Christ; but they kept hearing, 'He who once persecuted us is now preaching the faith which he once tried to destroy. And they were glorifying God because of me.'" (Galatians 1:22-24)

I wish I could pray Galatians 1:24 with the full confidence of Paul! Think about those words: they glorify God because of me. Have you ever considered that maybe part of the reason God gives you His favor is to glorify Himself and not yourself?

Before Paul encountered the risen Lord Jesus on the Damascus road, he was called Saul and public enemy number one of the Church. He was the point of the spear persecuting Christians until God knocked him off his high horse (literally) with a voice from heaven. Jesus told Saul, "You are fighting for the wrong team! You are not persecuting heretics. You are persecuting God." Saul was standing in the way and attempting to block God's plans and favor!

Saul's radical conversion became a catalyst for the Jesus movement in the decades after Jesus' resurrection. And it was as obvious as Saul's name change that God's favor was all over Paul. But it wasn't easy. He suffered a lot.

Read the book of Acts. Paul was shipwrecked, bitten by a poisonous viper, beaten publicly, and put in prison. Every time he faced a trial, Paul used it as a way to Tell Them of Him—a value of ours at Faith Promise. When in prison, Paul worshipped God. And when an earthquake rocked that prison and the doors opened, Paul remained and led the jailer and his family to Jesus. Paul stood before kings, queens, civic and religious leaders and boldly proclaimed Jesus and His resurrection from the dead.

Problems plagued Paul throughout his ministry. However, with every problem came miracles, signs, and the supernatural. Sure, he faced trials, but God's favor was already at work and flowed through Paul every time.

Don't see your problems as God having abandoned you!

Instead, look at problems as an opportunity for God's glory to shine through you. I wish every Promisor could live Galatians 1:24 so others would glorify God because of you.

Robbie's Story

"But Dad, what do I say?" Eli said. It was Fusion weekend and I had challenged Eli to share the gospel with a seventh grader who raised his hand for prayer.

"Just talk to him about Jesus," I said.

Eli headed off to talk to the boy. Later in the day, I stood among a group of student leaders recapping stories from the service.

"Can you believe the high school boy who shared the gospel with our student this morning? Man, he was like a little pastor," said one a leader.

Someone smacked me on the arm, "He is talking about your boy, Robbie. That was Eli." I couldn't hold back the tears. I can't remember a time when I was prouder of my eldest son. The following day he and I dropped off the other tenth grade boys back at their homes. As soon as the last kid was dropped off, Eli sat up in his seat and turned off the radio. He looked at me with sheer excitement.

"Dad, I have to tell you something," said Eli, "Dad, it wasn't me who was talking!"

"What do you mean?" I asked.

"When I walked back into the room to talk to that boy about Jesus. I didn't know what to say. So, I just prayed, "Spirit, please help me." After that, it wasn't me talking! I mean, I was saying the words, so I was talking, but I wasn't thinking of the words. It was like the words were written down in front of my eyes, and I was just reading them," said Eli.

My arms were covered in goosebumps. What happened that weekend is something Eli will never forget. He knows God is there. He knows God speaks to us and can speak through us. He knows God is always at work!

Robbie Freeman is the Pastor of Groups and Missions at the North Knoxville Campus and contributed greatly in helping me put together this devotional.

Faith Declaration

Today I will view every problem as an opportunity for God's favor to work in me and through me. People who know me will glorify God because of His favor on me and in me. I will see life from God's perspective, not my own. I am a tool in the top drawer ready to be used as God sees fit.

Question + Response

What is an event or an occasion in your life that led people to glorify God because of you?

What could God be calling you to do so more people might glorify Him?

Prayers answered

Grateful for

How did God move?

— Day Thirteen —
HEAVY GLORY

Kavod

Heavy Glory

"But we all, with unveiled face, beholding as in a mirror the glory of the Lord, are being transformed into the same image from glory to glory, just as from the Lord, the Spirit."
– 2 Corinthians 3:18

Daily Devotion

As Christ followers, the weighty glory of God is available to us. We can walk under an open heaven like warriors, but we must first realize and recognize who we are in Christ. If we walk in defeat, discouragement, or with a downcast spirit, we will miss what the Lord desires.

So how can we walk and look toward our Heavenly Father to please Him?

The psalmist writes in Psalm 34:5, "They looked to Him and were radiant. And their faces will never be ashamed."

The faces of the those who stand for God are radiant with joy. We are citizens of the Kingdom of God and we are marked for heaven. We should be the happiest people on the planet! We are raised from the dead. The world should see an overflowing outpouring of joy in our attitudes and actions.

Paul writes a reminder to "Speak to one another in psalms and hymns and spiritual songs, singing and making melody with your heart to the Lord. Always giving thanks for all things in the name of our Lord Jesus Christ to God." (Ephesians 5:19-20)

Once the favor of God falls in our lives, like a catchy song, we can't help but sing the tune and whistle along.

Favor should add density to your destiny.

God's favor at work should be an anchoring force marking the people of God and aiding our walks here on earth. Favor gives us an advantage in all we do for the King of Heaven. God's favor, like His glory, is weighty or heavy.

A biblical definition for glory is, "the heavy presence of God." If you believe it and go looking for it, the heavy favor of God can rest on you as a mark of God. No matter who, what, when, or where you came from, once you become a follower of Christ, you are part of God's family and fellow heirs with His Chosen Son, Jesus. (Romans 8:16-17)

So even when we suffer, we are not alone and we will not see our stories end there. Because God keeps His own. And the weighty glory and favor of God is waiting, working, and available both now and forever.

Jody's Story

Last year, I experienced the power and beauty of God's presence in a unique way.

For two years, my mom battled cancer and it was time for the end of the journey. We are a tight-knit family. There are four children and we loved our mom deeply. She was an amazing mom and great "Mamaw" to her grandchildren. She truly was one of a kind.

Most importantly, Mom's faith in Jesus was strong. Her love for Christ not only shaped her faith but all of ours as well. Hospice care began in January of 2019 and she won her battle with cancer in March, graduating to her real home in Glory.

There were several times during her last days when we sat surrounding her bed. We prayed, played her favorite hymns, and cried. After the funeral, each of our families privately said a final earthly goodbye at her casket.

When my husband, Brian, the kids, and I made our way to her, something overwhelmed me. I was overcome with the heavy presence of the Lord. I prayed with my kids and thanked God for her life and legacy and the incredible blessing and favor of God for giving our family the gift of a mom and Mamaw like her.

I miss Mom every day, but I am thankful for God's never-ending presence. He continually reminds me Mom's best day is every day in eternity!

If I'm honest, there are times I don't feel the full weight of God's presence, but when I stop to consider why not, I realize because I'm distracted. While there can be many distractions and noises in our lives, God's favor never stops working.

What are the distractions keeping you from seeing God's favor at work or feeling the heavy presence of God? When was the last time God moved your heart, changed your course, or gave you lasting peace about a real problem?

Jody Kenyon is my executive assistant and is a lifetime Promisor, serving the people of Faith Promise faithfully for over 20 years with first the Groups ministry and now in the Executive office.

Faith Declaration

God's glory and favor will rest heavily on me today. I will reject my past perspective and feel the full weight of how God views me. I will walk under an open heaven and allow His favor to be a force for the future.

Question + Response

Think of times you have felt the *kavod* of God's glory or times God sucked the air out of the room on your behalf. Write down and spend some time meditating on those memories or special moments.

Prayers answered

Grateful for

How did God move?

REAL PEOPLE

> "God is able to make all grace abound to you,
> so that always having all sufficiency in everything,
> you may have an abundance for every good deed."
> – 2 Corinthians 9:8

Daily Devotion

Peter was one of Jesus' closest friends. He left everything and followed Jesus for three years. However, after Peter saw Jesus come back from the grave, he was a changed man. Peter spent the rest of his life preaching the Good News of Jesus' life and death on a Roman cross to the world.

> "Beloved, do not be surprised at the fiery ordeal among you, which comes upon you for your testing, as though some strange thing were happening to you; but to the degree that you share the sufferings of Christ, keep on rejoicing." – 1 Peter 4:12-13

Fiery ordeal? Testing? Suffering? This doesn't sound like good news at all!

So, what about the times God allows us to walk through difficult circumstances? Peter encourages us, "Don't freak out when you experience real problems, they are going to happen."

With God's favor, we gain heaven's perspective, which can change our lives for the better, even if the circumstances don't change right away. Let's be real! You know this is true. More often than not, we focus on our immediate circumstances with little regard for how the Lord is already working.

Trials, problems, and pain do not mean God has abandoned you.

Dangerous trials not only happened in ancient history, they still happen today.

In January of 2020, a terrorist group called Boko Haram beheaded Reverend Lawan Andimi, a Nigerian pastor. Why was he killed? Because he refused to renounce his Christian faith.

Being in the center of God's will is not always safe or comfortable. But the favor of God is an incredible force, because favor moves God's Kingdom forward no matter what happens.

Vikki's Story

It was a Saturday morning about twenty years ago. And I remember waking up, full of joy! I had recently given birth to a baby named Josh. Jacob, his older brother, adored the new baby and my amazing husband Rick was still home on paternity leave. Everything was perfect.

After breakfast, I headed to the bathroom to "put on my face." I put my left contact lens comfortably in place, and then I moved on to the right. But something was off. No matter what I did, the contact would not stay in my eye. Thinking it was defective, I tossed it and tried a new lens. It still wouldn't stay in my eye. I called for Rick. When I opened my mouth to speak, my right cheek went numb. My bottom lip drooped and I could barely form words with my mouth. I thought, "What is happening to me? I am 27 years old. I can't be having a stroke, can I?"

We went to the emergency room right away, where a doctor diagnosed me with Bell's Palsy. In short, a nerve in my face was on the fritz and caused temporary facial paralysis. Nobody knows the cause of Bell's Palsy and there is no definitive treatment and no prognosis on how long it will last.

During the next couple of years, it felt like Bell's Palsy controlled my life. Sometimes I had to hold my bottom lip up to a glass with my left hand when I took a drink. Sometimes, to my embarrassment, I drooled. There were nights when I had to tape my eye closed to sleep. And there were days where it felt like someone was hammering a railroad spike into my skull.

I felt unfit to take care of my children. I was embarrassed and ashamed. In my depression, I convinced myself that someone would take my boys away from me. Rick held me many nights while I sobbed from the pain and sadness. One night I prayed. I mean, I prayed really hard. I begged God to take away Bell's Palsy from me.

God gave a clear answer that night. For some people, maybe that happens a lot. But for me, it's the only time I know for sure that I heard the voice of God.

He said, "I'll heal you, but not completely. And it will be on My time frame, not yours."

Over time I improved, and to the naked eye, I appear back to my old self. Today, the palsy is still there. My eyes are not entirely in sync, and when the weather gets cold, the right side of my mouth feels numb. Once in a while, when I get overwhelmed and refuse to ask for help, the symptoms return.

I'm inclined to think that this is one of the reasons God said He wouldn't heal me completely. It is a reminder to depend on Him daily, and not myself. But I know no matter what, God is still at work and working in me.

Vikki Huisman is a lifelong resident of Illinois and a virtual assistant at Faith Promise. She and her husband of over 20 years, Rick, have three sons. Vikki enjoys serving as a children's ministry volunteer at her church in Illinois.

Faith Declaration

Today, I will see Christ before I see my circumstances. The Lord will use me no matter where I find myself today. Your favor will be a force in my life. You will open heaven and pour out Your favor. I will stand in the will of God and the world will never be the same.

Question + Response

What is something you are wrestling with God about in your life? Write it down and have a real conversation with Him about it today.

Prayers answered

Grateful for

How did God move?

REAL PROBLEMS

> "Rejoice always; pray without ceasing;
> in everything give thanks;
> for this is God's will for you in Christ Jesus."
> – 1 Thessalonians 5:16-18

Daily Devotion

"Pastor Chris, I wish my circumstances could change, but…"

"I know the Lord blesses others, but there is no way out of my situation!"

Can I be real with you? Get rid of that stinkin' thinkin'!

God gave us a copy of His Heart in the Bible. In the Old Testament, we see the shapes and shadows of things to come. The more you know the Word, the more prepared you are to face real problems.

A man named Job can teach us a lot about living in hellacious circumstances. In one day, Job went from filthy rich and feasting, to dirt poor and starving. Job lost all his money *and* all his children to tragic deaths.

At his lowest, Job did wonder if he was alone. Had God left him? Where were his real friends and his wife? Job begged to die because he no longer felt the force of favor. Job didn't deserve what happened to him. He wasn't harboring some secret sin or stepping outside of God's will.

Despite all of the horrible events unfolding, Job never cursed God. At one point in the tenth chapter of the book of Job, he says, "I know God has granted me favor," even though Job would not appear to feel God's favor return for another thirty-three chapters!

Most of us feel forsaken in times of difficulty, and in those times it's easy to forget God's favor. It's easy to focus on the obstacles, problems, mountains, and people hurting us or blocking our path. But when we rely on the knowledge that God is at work, we will be able to walk in His favor even when we don't feel it.

And here's some good news: God is always at work!

God is always pushing back the darkness to make room for the joy that will come in the morning. What feels and looks like a problem tonight, God will use to promote you tomorrow.

In the darkest night, Job had no idea tomorrow would bring back twice what he thought he had lost. Because even the children Job lost he would see again. Nothing is lost forever on God's watch.

Maybe you're like Job. Your problems are not a sign of God turning His back on you. Maybe God is setting you up for your future or a new season of favor. This is why we must continue to focus on God and His favor, no matter what!

Kandice's Story

Sometimes life can be excruciating. Sometimes life can be painful. Sometimes life just seems unfair.

One summer, some years back, I lost a baby boy. He was stillborn. Four months later, on Thanksgiving, I miscarried another baby. The hurt, the disappointment, the numbness, the anger—no combination of words seem to be powerful enough to describe the agony.

Doctors diagnosed me with a blood clotting disorder which causes my body to lose babies. So, I did the only thing I knew to do—worship Jesus.

I cried out to God through tears at night alone in my living room. I sat with the Bible in one hand and a pen in the other. I journaled my thoughts and consumed Bible verses about healing, children, faith, and motherhood. As I wrote and read and prayed and cried one verse stood out.

"Truly I say to you, whoever says to this mountain, 'Be taken up and cast into the sea,' and does not doubt in his heart, but believes that what he says is going to happen, it will be granted him." (**Mark 11:23**).

Many nights I sat alone with God and prayed this scripture over my body. Somewhere, while praying, crying, and speaking God's Word out loud, His Word came to life in my spirit. Like an instant revelation, my focus shifted from babies to God. Like Pastor shared early in this devotional, we are to go after *God*, not His blessings. We follow the Father, not His favor!

Because, can I tell you something? Our God is BIG. Not only did He answer my cries, He answered five times (including twins) with Ashley, Michael, Whitney, Ben, and Alex—my five living miracles of His favor.

What do you need to do today to see through the storm and see how God is working?

Kandice Baker leads faithfully at Faith Promise as our fpKIDS pastor at North Knox, along with her husband Pastor Mike. Both have served on staff for years and their children volunteer alongside them at the North Knox Campus.

Faith Declaration

Today, I believe God will burst on the scene. The problems holding me back will be what God uses to promote me. I will worship the Lord, and my adoration, attention, and focus will remain on Him and His limitless power.

Question + Response

Imagine you have a friend struggling to make sense of the tremendous suffering in the world. The struggle is hindering her from pursuing a relationship with God. How would you approach her? What would you say?

Prayers answered

Grateful for

How did God move?

— Day Sixteen —
IMPOSSIBLE

"Call to Me and I will answer you, and I will tell you great and mighty
things, which you do not know."
– Jeremiah 33:3

Daily Devotion

God's favor marks His children, but sometimes His mark
can seem hidden. Remember, favor is a force of God at work
whether we see it or not. Throughout the Scriptures, the
children of God often acted out of fear in times when God's
mark of favor appeared hidden. We read stories in Exodus,
Numbers, and Judges, and wonder, "Why didn't they just
have faith?"

But if we're being real, we struggle in the same ways.

In Exodus 14, Pharaoh and his army of chariots cornered
the Israelites against the Red Sea and there was no way
out. With mountains on both sides, the Red Sea in front,
and Pharaoh's furious army bearing down on them, bent
on payback for the plagues, everything looked hopeless.
Terrified, God's people just knew Egypt was going to
slaughter the men and re-enslave the women and children.
Have you experienced a Red Sea moment in your life? How
did you respond?

Read the story in Exodus 14 if you don't know how it ends.
It's awesome!

One minute, death and defeat is bearing down on them.
The next, they are rejoicing watching the death and defeat

of their enemies. God's favor can flip the fear within us and the odds around us, even in the midst of the impossible.

"If we are faithless, He remains faithful,
for He cannot deny Himself."
– 2 Timothy 2:13

When you look around at your life, do you see the mountains closing in around you? Do you see pain, problems, and impossible circumstances? Do you see no way out? Your enemy does not get the last move because God is always moving. He is not limited by our lack of sight, limited vision, or lean faith. He loves you and will bring His best to bear. So the next time you feel surrounded, trust Him.

Tony's Story

Around ten years ago, my family took a vacation on a cruise ship. It was our last day on the water and we were sailing back to port near the coast of Miami. Everyone was relaxing and enjoying the last few hours we had left. As my brother and mom sat in one of the dining rooms eating lunch, my brother suddenly leaned back and lost consciousness.

Mom shouted for help, but in the fifteen minutes it took for the medical team to arrive, my brother's heart had stopped beating. After four shocks with an A.E.D. (Automated External Defibrillator), my brother, once again, had a pulse.

The team rushed him away on a stretcher and although he looked unconscious, he was screaming. The doctor pulled the family aside and warned us that my brother had gone a long period of time without a pulse, and even if he regained consciousness, he was probably going to have severe brain damage. So, I immediately contacted our church family.

"Pray for a miracle," I begged them.

Within minutes, hundreds of people were praying for a miracle for my brother. I prayed, believing in faith, even though all hope seemed lost. An hour later, a rescue boat from Miami took my brother to Jackson Memorial Hospital.

Eventually, he regained consciousness. But here's the miraculous part...there was NO brain damage. After some tests, my brother was diagnosed with a very rare heart disease called Brugada Syndrome, which causes a disruption of the heart's normal rhythm.

In a true mark of God's blessing and favor, one of the world specialists in Brugada Syndrome just happened to work at Jackson Memorial Hospital! Today, I can happily share that my brother is alive and in excellent health.

I know stories like this seem hard to believe sometimes. At the time of the accident, a show called Danger Coast was being broadcast on CMT and you can watch the actual rescue boat exchange with my brother on season one, episode four.

Tony and his wife are faithful Promisors and he serves on staff for the Global Operations Team in IT. He is an aspiring Spikeball player who plans to turn pro someday because nothing is impossible.

Faith Declaration

Today, I will focus on the limitless power of my God. Even when I see no way out, my God's perfect vision will guide me through today and into eternity. I will trust and rest in His Mighty Hands no matter what!

Question + Response

What is something that seems impossible in your life? How could your belief for God's favor in this impossibility mark your life?

_____

_____

_____

_____

Read 1 John 2:28-3:10. What are some of the markings of a child of God?

_____

_____

_____

_____

Prayers answered

Grateful for

How did God move?

—— Day Seventeen ——
INSECURITY

**"For God gave us a spirit not of fear
but of power, love, and self-control."
– 2 Timothy 1:7 (ESV)**

Daily Devotion

Do you ever find yourself in the Christian comparison game? Do you find yourself looking at people who God seems to be using more and blessing more and wondering if they have more of God's favor than you do? Can I tell you something?

God favors you. And God has plans for you.

Yes, He knows your flaws. Yes, He knows where you messed up. But He has chosen you for His particular purpose. Do not fall into the trap of Christian comparison. If you do, you might accidentally opt-out of serving Him all together.

Most of the Hall of Fame of Faith people in Hebrews 11 made excuses and asked God to use someone else first. When we doubt ourselves and dwell on our own shortcomings, we disqualify ourselves even when God desires to use us. In the Old Testament, we find someone who was just like us in this way.

Gideon was saturated in insecurity and bogged down with excuses. Let's get raw and real: how many times have you made excuses when God called you to do something? They may have sounded something like these:

"God, I don't have the gifting, ability, connections, or experience."

"God, I'm not good enough, smart enough, spiritual enough."

"God, listen, you've got the wrong person."

Moses did the same thing. Read his conversation with God in Exodus 4. Like him, too many of us fail to focus on God's favor. He desires to "confirm the work of our hands." That's why Psalm 90:17 is our theme verse for the year. He sends His favor not only to mark you, but to confirm the work of your hands!

While Gideon was wondering why God did not do something about the Midianites robbing them blind, God said, "I'll use you." What do you think Gideon's reply was?

"Alright God! I'll go!"
"Great! I'm ALL iN!"
"Look out Midianites, here comes God's servant, Gideon!"

Nope, Gideon said, "I'm the least person in the nation."

Can you believe it?

Gideon tried telling God he should be God's last pick on the team. Instead of looking and seeing how God was at work, Gideon hung his head instead, completely unable to see how God could use him.

Like Gideon, how many of us choose to just hide in a cave and be content with whatever the enemy leaves us? How many of us have answered a call from God just like Gideon?

"I can't do it."
"There is no hope for me."
"Anybody would be better than me. I've tried before."

Promisor, God and His favor are at work in you and through you! You are a favored child of God and He is about to use you for great things. God has a purpose for your life. He has an aim to bring glory to His name and you have a part to play.

It is time to pay attention to how God is moving. It is time to lean into faith, step up, and tell God, "Here I am. Pick me!" His favor is on you, but you'll never experience the fullness of His favor in life without stepping out in faith.

Faith Declaration

Today, I will walk in the grace and mercy God has given me. I'm not perfect, but God will use me for His glory. I will not disqualify myself from His miracles. His blessing and favor will confirm the work of my hands today.

Question + Response

What common excuses do you use to avoid serving the
Lord?

At Faith Promise, one of our values is *We Serve Others.* How
and where are you serving others?

What insecurities do you need to let go of? Jesus follower,
you are not meant to carry these fears and doubts anymore.
Let them go and watch them sink into the deep depths of
your past.

Prayers answered

Grateful for

How did God move?

WALLS OF PROTECTION

> "'For I,' declares the Lord, 'will be a wall of fire around her,
> and I will be the glory in her midst.'"
> – Zechariah 2:5

Daily Devotion

Moses recorded this verse as God was telling the Israelites of His Glory and Presence at work in their very midst. This verse is also one I pray over my family day after day, year after year because I believe God's favor builds a wall around us. Stop and take a minute to pray this verse over your family right now:

> **"God, be a wall of fire around my family.**
> **Be the glory in our midst."**

Last week, I mentioned the plagues in Egypt a couple of times, but did you know that each plague proved God's power over different idols? It's true. We often overlook something amazing recorded in Exodus: each plague was a targeted attack on the Egyptian gods, but none of the plagues God sent against Egypt touched Goshen.

Goshen was the community where the Hebrew people lived. Through all the plagues, not a single stray fly, locust, frog, or rock of hail landed there. Talk about favor! And even more miraculously, they did not lose a single firstborn child. God's wall of protection, even amid all heaven breaking loose, was visible to everyone around—even those far from God.

No matter what you're experiencing, God can build a wall of protection around you. He can build a wall around your marriage, your kids, your finances, your health, and your future. Do you believe in this kind of favorable protection?

Time after time during the Exodus, the children of God were fearful and without faith—but God! Close to two million Hebrews walked free. God sustained them with food and water in the wilderness and built a literal wall of fire for them to follow at night. Imagine what He can do in your life!

Do you believe in God's life-changing power? Do you believe Him for a wall of fire? Israel was a nation of God's children. Don't you want to do everything you can for your kids? Every time God blesses you or builds a wall for you, give Him all the glory so others will glorify Him because of you. So, even if you feel like you are drowning, God can make a wall of water so you can walk on dry land to safety.

Kayla's Story

There weren't any family devotionals at my house growing up.

My parents and brothers suffered from severe alcoholism and drug addiction. It seemed like every night there was a crowd of drunk people right outside my bedroom door at all hours, like a frat party.

My home felt like a warzone and I never felt safe.

When I hid in my room at night, I vowed to never let my children go through the things I went through. Sometimes, I even spent the night at my friend's house just to get away.

When I was fifteen, my friend invited me to her church. This was when I learned God is really there and working all the time. This is where I learned He is my Heavenly Father and He favors and loves me. Despite the hurt and brokenness I experienced in my earthly family, God protected me until I could get away from the toxic environment.

God's favor put so many people into my life through the church. People who took me in and loved me deeply. God even blessed me with several "adopted" parents.

His favor was at work and protected me through horrible circumstances, even before I really knew Him. He's healed me, made me whole, and brought me to where I am today.

And I believe through His blessings and favor that He broke generational curses. Today I am a wife and a mother to an amazing family that I adore!

How has your life turned out differently because of God's protection?

Kayla Hanna and her husband, Adam, recently moved to Tennessee and became part of the Faith Promise family. Kayla serves as the Executive Assistant to Worship.

Faith Declaration

Today, the Lord is a wall of fire around me. His glory and favor are on me and my family. I will stand in God's promised protection and walk with Him. No weapon formed against me will prosper. I will stand my ground for God. I am strong and armed for battle.

Question + Response

Write down a memory from a time God protected you.
Thank Him for His wall of protection surrounding you!

Prayers answered

Grateful for

How did God move?

— Day Nineteen —
IN THE FIRE

"Bless those who persecute you; bless and do not curse. Rejoice with
those who rejoice, and weep with those who weep."
– Romans 12:14-15

Daily Devotion

We keep it raw and real at Faith Promise. But you know
what? Jesus kept it raw and real two thousand years before
we did. He told His followers, **"In the world, you will have
tribulation." (John 16:33)**

We live in a cursed world and the consequences of sin affect
us all. You can be the most faith-filled, spiritual person in the
world, but you are still going to face tribulations, trials, and
times of testing.

The best way to prepare for these times of testing is to build
up your faith and equip your mind *before* the temperature
turns up. Don't have that stinkin' thinkin' like Job's friends.
Job's peanut gallery said he "lost" all of God's favor when
trials came his way. However, when we read the New
Testament, it is clear that Jesus' favored followers faced all
kinds of trials and testing.

Matthew 8 records a literal storm which struck his disciples
as they sailed on the Sea of Galilee. And how did Jesus
react? He was calm, cool, and collecting some zzz's (Greek
for taking a nap). The storm did not catch Jesus off guard.

When you think of God's favor, do you only imagine times
of success and blessings?

It's easy for most of us to believe in times of plenty, but what about in times of drought? What about when the storms come or the heat turns up and we begin to doubt? Remember, whether it's lousy news, blown opportunities, or missed goals, God has not forsaken or forgotten you.

Look for the miracle and how God is at work just beyond the horizon.

God's favor can cover you even in the storm, even in addiction, even in disease, and yes, even in failure. **"You surround him with favor as with a shield." (Psalm 5:12)** You may have been through a horrible divorce, a tough bankruptcy, or even devastating tragedy. But the truth is, none of this catches God off guard.

God and His favor never stop working.

In Daniel 3, we read about three young men who refused to turn their backs on God and worship an idol. The notorious King Nebuchadnezzar was furious and told them, "If you do not worship the idol, you shall immediately be cast into a burning fiery furnace. And who is the god who will deliver you out of my hands?"

From a place of favor and faith, Shadrach, Meshach, and Abednego responded, "Our God, who we serve, can deliver us from the burning fiery furnace."

The King was hot with anger and made sure those boys were going to feel his wrath. "Put more wood on the fire," he said. "More wood. Bigger flames." The fire was so massive it killed some of his own men who were *outside* the furnace. Then he ordered the three young men thrown into the fire.

When the King and his counselors looked into the raging furnace, they were shocked to see a fourth person. The person walking with the three young men protected them and onlookers described the fourth as having the appearance of "a son of the gods." If I could spiritually speculate, I think the person in the fire was a Christophany, which is just a fancy Old Testament word for a sneak peek of God's Son, Jesus.

So, if you find yourself in the fire today, good news— someone is there with you. Don't be anxious. Jesus is right there standing next to you. God is in control. When God's gold is in the fire, His Hand is on the thermostat. You are God's gold, His precious treasure. When you face the fire, trust God. He is ready to refine His favor in you for the whole world to see and so everyone can see His glory.

Faith Declaration

I will trust God no matter how high or hot the flames get that test me today.

I will walk in the favor of God. The trials I face today will be for my good and for His glory. Today, everything I think, say, and do will bring more glory to God!

Question + Response

What fires have you walked through in the past and what fires are you walking through right now? How might God be at work in refining you to reveal His Glory to those around you?

_____

_____

_____

_____

_____

_____

_____

Prayers answered

Grateful for

How did God move?

——— Day Twenty ———
KEYS

"For it is You who blesses the righteous man, O LORD,
You surround him with favor as with a shield."
– Psalm 5:12

Daily Devotion

How is your prayer life? If you are like most Christ followers, you will probably recognize it could use a little improvement. Want some help? Try praying through a chapter of the book of Psalms every day. Psalm 5 is one of those prayers you should keep on your mind all the time.

Ask God for favor at home, in your group, at school, at work, and in all your activities. Declare it throughout the day:

**"I have favor today like a shield.
God will move on my behalf."**

Declare favor for your kids at school, in their sports, with their health, and especially in their spiritual lives. This is not about "positive thinking." This is about declaring the promises of God.

In Proverbs 3:6 (TLB), wisdom challenges us, **"In everything you do, put God first, and He will direct you and crown your efforts with success."** In my life experience, the times when I put God first happened to also be the times I found unimaginable success and favor. Why is that?

Is it possible we sometimes put prayer in a box?

When we tuck the kids in at bedtime or mutter a prayer before a meal, it barely scratches the surface of the power of prayer. Prayer should be an interesting conversation with the One True God and a powerful moment with the Creator of the entire cosmos.

Last year, God stirred a spirit of revival in our church and hundreds of Promisors showed up on Saturday mornings for prayer gatherings across all our campuses. Those gatherings became living examples of the diversity, intensity, and potential of prayer.

Elders anointed the sick with oil, some prayed out loud, others sang, some walked, others laid down on the ground, and some journaled as they prayed. What an amazing time it is to see a room full of Promisors pounding on the door of the Throne Room together.

When I pray, I tell the Lord, "thank you for Your favor at work in me today." When you're favor-minded, you can agree with King David that the Lord's "goodness and loving kindness will follow me all the days of my life."

Not some days. All the days.

Make this a daily confession and declaration. The more you look for and thank God for favor, the more you'll recognize God at work in your life. Choose today to live with heavenly expectations of favor confirming the work of your hands.

I know a Promisor whose family was recently transplanted to Knoxville, 500 miles away from everything they knew. It was a stressful time, but their family had faith and knew God was in the transition.

One morning, this Promisor heard the radio DJ talking about Solomon and his wisdom. She started praying, "God, give my husband wisdom, discernment, and knowledge. God, set him on a course to find our new home in this new place." Later in the afternoon, her husband called excitedly because he had found a beautiful home. He retold the story of how he was driving around, looking for an apartment, but became lost and decided to turn around in a subdivision. He saw a house with a for sale sign and called the number.

On the phone, he told his wife, "I'm going to send you the address so you can see where it is. The address is on Wisdom Lane. It is on the corner of Wisdom and Knowledge." She then told him the story of how she had prayed for him to have knowledge in his search and for Godly wisdom like Solomon. "You're not going to believe this," he said. "This house is in Solomon Place subdivision!" They knew they had found their home.

God orders our steps and He provides for His children.

Faith Declaration

Today, I will see God's goodness and loving kindness chase me down. His blessings and favor will capture me and bring me back into the Throne Room of God. I will worship the Lord and look for His works and favor at every turn today. Others will see His favor on me and through me as I share Jesus with them.

Question + Response

We have an all-access backstage pass to God's Throne
Room. How much time do you spend taking advantage of
this amazing privilege?

What will be your keys to spending more time with God
in prayer?

Prayers answered

Grateful for

How did God move?

QUALIFIED

"And hearing this, Jesus said to them, 'It is not those who are healthy who
need a physician, but those who are sick;
I did not come to call the righteous, but sinners.'"
– Mark 2:17

Daily Devotion

Do you believe God has a plan and a purpose for your life?

Well, He does! And yet, how many times do we disqualify
ourselves from His bigger and better plans? When we
choose doubt, we forfeit favor before God can even move on
our behalf.

King David asked the Lord, "Who am I, O Lord GOD, and
what is my house, that You have brought me this far?" (**2
Samuel 7:18**) Remember all the way back to Day 7 when we
looked at how David was not supposed to become a King?
He had nothing going for him!

David's own family saw him as nothing more than a lowly
sheepherder. He didn't have an excellent education. He was
not rich. He definitely didn't have the pedigree to become
"the Man." David was not even looking for a promotion.
Instead, the promotion came to him.

God's favor works in amazing ways.

God can send incredible promotions and open doors you
may think you're not qualified to walk through. You may
not have the experience or education yet, but God's favor

can move you forward. Too many of us don't naturally look for favor and fall victim to the usual mind monsters with thoughts like:

"There is no way!"
"This won't happen for me."
"There are others better than me."

When you think with insecurity, you forfeit favor before it can even begin to flow. Push aside the mind monsters and allow God to take you from the back of the line to the front, from obscurity to visibility, from last to first.

For years, I went to church conferences and gatherings of pastors and leaders. I sat in the audience and wondered: "What are those people like? How do they think? What do they do in their time with God?"

Then God's favor moved! Now, I get the opportunity to speak to pastors and leaders across the world about King Jesus. Through God's favor He's blessed me with new connections, wise mentors, and taken me to places I never imagined.

Where might the Lord take you? What doors might He open for you? If God has given you a vision, His plans for you will begin working regardless of your background, family, or pedigree. Your future and destiny are not in the hands of others, they are in the hands of God.

Jamie's Story

Even in my darkest times of self-doubt and insecurity about my body image, God decided to use me. I felt so ashamed of my body, and deep down, I was most ashamed of myself. I felt unworthy. I used the scale for decades as the measure of success or failure in life. Most of the time, I was losing the battle with the scale, but when I look back, it is clear God was working and winning the battle in my heart first.

Then, God led me to Faith Promise where I was developed by great leaders, grew in my faith, found my real identity, and lost more than 160 pounds along the way. I'm forever grateful that God chose me and believed in me, even when I did not believe in myself.

I love people and being around them brings me life. I used to be the person that would hide in the corner, scared to death someone might notice me. Talking to a big crowd of people was a nightmare, not a dream!

But God's favor is real, and it moves you into places and positions you could never imagine. God uses me to build relationships and lead so many amazing people in fpKIDS and fpGroups. Sometimes I host our weekend services in front of huge crowds, speak on stage at fpCelebrate, and lead meetings for fpGroups.

The shy person hiding in the back of the room is now comfortable on the stage. Now, God regularly allows me to share my story and the story of my awesome kids. I now walk into a room covered in the full confidence of God's favor. Want to know the best part? I get to be me, the real me! The me God made me to be and called out before I even believed!

Jamie Davis, his wife Stephanie, and their kids Lily, Jordy, and Daisy are a beautiful example of God's desire and design for a family. Jamie serves on staff as Associate Pastor of Groups and Missions at the Pellissippi Campus. Over the course of a year, Jamie lost over 160 pounds and is living proof of God's favor at work.

Faith Declaration

Today, God will open doors I cannot open for myself. I may not be qualified yet, but God is my source of favor and He will endorse me as He sees fit. No one can thwart the plans God has for me. I will not forfeit favor through lack of faith. I will not disqualify myself from anything God desires for me.

Question + Response

God made you with strengths, values, and spiritual gifts. What would you see if you took an X-ray of your unique design?

_____

_____

_____

If time and money were not an option, what would you do?

_____

_____

_____

Prayers answered

Grateful for

How did God move?

— Day Twenty-Two —
BLESSINGS

"Search me, O God, and know my heart;
Try me and know my anxious thoughts;
And see if there be any hurtful way in me,
And lead me in the everlasting way."
– Psalm 139:23-24

Daily Devotion

Look at the world around you. Check Facebook, Instagram, and the news. Doesn't it feel like we live in a hyper-negative world? Negativity is easy because it is natural. Relentless positivity is supernatural.

Having faith and finding favor should lead to living with a positive outlook, which is a gift from God. Remember all the way back to Day 2 of this devotional and what Balaam said to Balak,

"How shall I curse whom God has not cursed?"
– Numbers 23:8

And while this means the enemy and others *can't* curse you, you absolutely can curse yourself! Negative self-talk, or what the Bible calls "speaking death" (**Proverbs 18:21**), leads to a pessimistic life without favor. And whether you recognize it or not, you will begin to subconsciously bring your life into line with what you speak and believe of yourself.

What if someone followed you around the entire day with a device recording all your thoughts and words? At the end of the day, if you played back the recording, I think you would be shocked.

How many negative words do we curse ourselves with every single day?

Day by day, we curse our future and forget about God's favor. The devil doesn't need to stop us. Maybe one of the reasons we don't find favor is because we stop ourselves from looking for God. But here's some good news! God *is* looking for us. And He is looking to bless us, give us favor, and open doors!

A pastor I know once looked at me and said, "Chris, the Lord blesses you, but not me." I rebuked him in Jesus' name and shared with him all the Lord could do, but he refused to believe me. It breaks my heart to share that today, he's divorced and out of ministry. He cut himself out and off from all God wanted to do in him and through him. Don't let that become true of you.

God is working right now for your good and His Glory and His plans are always the best. Let me challenge you to walk in joy, peace, and victory today and read the blessing below over your family. It is a blessing straight from God's Word. Declare his favor over your life and choose to live in faith today.

"The Lord bless you and keep you;
the Lord make his face to shine upon you
and be gracious to you;
the Lord lift up his countenance upon you
and give you peace."
– Numbers 6:24-26

Faith Declaration

Today, I will speak life, not death. I will believe God for greater things. I will refuse to curse myself with negative self-talk, and instead proclaim God's preferred future for me. I will be like Balaam and speak only of God's abundant blessing.

Question + Response

If you were to weigh your words on the scale of life or death, which side would the scale tip toward? Who in your life tips the scales towards speaking life and blessings into you?

Write some words that you should and shouldn't use to describe yourself on each side of the scale below.

Prayers answered

Grateful for

How did God move?

DREAMS

"The LORD will accomplish what concerns me."
– Psalm 138:8

Daily Devotion

What dreams are dead or dying in your life? Isn't it sad how quickly we give up on dead or dying dreams and goals that God has given to us? Throughout the Bible, there are countless stories and examples of those who never gave up on their God-given dreams. Throughout the Scriptures, we are encouraged and challenged to find resolve, resilience, grit, and endurance through the filling and favor of the Lord.

**Christ followers never give up because
we never stop believing.**

Faith is the assurance of things hoped for and the conviction of things not seen (Hebrews 11:1). Still, sometimes our hearts get broken. We lose someone close to us or someone betrays our trust. We lose a house or a job. We lose hope. When we experience these pains and problems, they begin to chip away at our belief and rot our resilience, leaving us with less faith than before.

Eventually, we settle. It is what it is. We are who we are.

And God's hopes and dreams for us slowly dissolve, disappear, and die. Remember, it is the Lord who controls your destiny, not people or circumstances. So, we must never forget or neglect to look and see God's favor at work.

Because if we look for it with God's help, we will find it.

God refuses to abort the dreams He's placed in your heart. We can walk out on those dreams but He never will. But let's be real. If it feels like you missed the moment and the time has passed, hope can begin to dwindle.

"Hope is lost."

That's what Sarah believed about having a baby in her later years.

That's what Mary and Martha believed when Lazarus died and was buried.

That's what the widow said at her son's funeral procession when Jesus arrived.

That's what the lame beggar told Peter and John at the foot of the Temple.

That's what the disciples said the night the Messiah was crucified on the cross.

All of these people, and so many more, had lost hope and almost given up. Think about the joy, the life, the restoration, the healing, and the freedom they would have missed out on!

God resurrects the dead dreams of His children.

Because God is always working and always pouring out His blessings and favor, we can be sure that there is always hope. He can add His favor to the work of your hands and make possible the impossible. He has supernatural dreams for you.

Faith Declaration

Today, I will walk in faith to do the impossible. I refuse to give up on my God-given dreams or settle for less than God promises. I will never count out the limitless authority, ability, and power of God at work in my life.

Question + Response

What are some God-given dreams you may have left for dead? How could God's blessings and favor still be at work and are you ready to resurrect them?

_____

_____

_____

_____

_____

_____

_____

What Dreams Are You Growing?

(Write them below)

Prayers answered

Grateful for

How did God move?

RISE

> "Now to Him who is able to do far more abundantly beyond all that we ask or think, according to the power that works within us."
> – Ephesians 3:20

Daily Devotion

Looking back at yesterday, what God-given dreams were dead because you thought they were impossible? Are you starting to believe again? If you are still struggling, look for ways God's favor could already be at work.

Our God is a miracle worker.

What we see as impossible is possible with God because His view is eternal.

In John 11, all Mary and Martha could see was an earthly view of their brother Lazarus dying. It's easy to sit back and judge, but when we look closer, we see how their family was among Jesus' closest friends and followers. That is why, when Lazarus' condition worsened, the sisters sent a messenger to find Jesus. Their message was simple:

"Jesus, come heal our brother."

Mary and Martha knew Jesus loved them and their brother. They believed Jesus could still heal Lazarus. They believed in Jesus' ability. So, when Jesus didn't come right away, Mary and Martha's work of sending the message looked to be in vain. And not only did Jesus *not* come right away, but Lazarus died.

A few days after Lazarus' death, Jesus says to the disciples, "Let's go back to Judea." The apostles are incredulous. *Not a good plan, Jesus.* (The last time they were in Judea, a bunch of the Jewish leaders tried to kill Jesus.) Despite their protests, the apostles and Jesus head back to Judea anyway.

When Jesus finally arrives, the sisters are broken-hearted. In fact, only Martha comes out to meet Jesus. Mary stays home and when she finally sees Jesus she cries, "If only you had been here, Jesus."

Their belief was buried. Their hope of healing was gone. Their brother was dead. Their dream of Jesus healing Lazarus might as well have been laid to rest in the tomb next to Lazarus. Let's be real, though—can you blame Mary and Martha?!

When they sent Jesus the message, Lazarus was still alive. Four days later when Jesus finally shows up, Lazarus is dead, buried, and in a tomb. Then Jesus says something to the sisters no one expects, "Your brother will rise again." And you know what happens next. In the midst of doubt, disbelief, and disappeared hope, Jesus says, "Lazarus, come out."

And just like that, the four-day-dead man gets up and walks out.

Whether you've given up on being healed, graduating school, getting married, having a child, getting promoted, or being set free from a stronghold—never lose hope. Hope is alive anywhere and anytime God is at work. Here is some truth for you:

God is *always* at work.

God sees you and He knows everything He's put in your heart. It is never too late, too hard, or too difficult for God. If He can speak the universe into existence and speak a dead man back to life, He can mostly definitely speak blessings and favor into your life, marriage, ministry, career, and calling.

Rachel's Story

I'll never forget lying on the bathroom floor of a hotel room, away from my husband and my community, begging God to resurrect the little life growing inside of me. After two miscarriages, I never dreamed I would face another.

It was a Sunday afternoon. I was eight weeks pregnant and exhausted from an early morning and busy afternoon when the bleeding began. I knew from the two previous losses what it meant and instantly began to weep.

Zac ran into the bathroom and found his crying wife... the moment was anything but beautiful. He prayed the obligatory prayer for God to heal, but our hearts cried betrayal.

Then, the Holy Spirit stirred Zac to pray for the baby to be restored, for every cell and membrane and piece to be made new. I would love to tell you how I joined him in belief, but I did not. I trust God, I love the Lord, but what's the point in asking for something impossible again?

Grieving the loss of another baby at the doctor's office the next day, I was frustrated by Zac's faith and his seeming dismissal of my anguish. But when the baby's heartbeat appeared on the screen during the exam, all I could hear were Jesus' words in **Matthew 8:26:**

"You of little faith, why are you so afraid?"

Our son, Elisha River, was born seven months later. The baby I miscarried. The baby I grieved. The baby I was too afraid to ask God to make alive again. Don't let loss, the world, or anything else rob you of the joy of asking your Heavenly Father for anything.

It's never too late.

And even if He says no once, it doesn't mean He will say no the next time. I'll always ask God, even if He says no once more. Even if I feel like it's too late. Even if it feels impossible. Because no matter what, God is always at work.

Pastor Zac and Rachel Stephens met as students at Faith Promise and are now married with three beautiful children. They have served together in fpStudents, as well as at the Farragut and Blount Campuses.

Faith Declaration

Today, I will believe God holds resurrection power in His Hand. He will bring dead bones to life and turn hearts of stone to hearts of flesh. Today, I will walk with an eternal expectancy of all my Heavenly Father will do.

Question + Response

Take a moment and read **Ephesians 3:20**, then pray it over your life today.

"Now to him who can do far more abundantly than all that we ask or think, according to the power at work within us, to Him be the glory in the church and in Christ Jesus throughout all generations, forever and ever."

Prayers answered

Grateful for

How did God move?

MAJORITY

"'Do not fear, for I am with you; Do not anxiously look about you, for I am your God. I will strengthen you, surely I will help you, surely I will uphold you with My righteous right hand.'"

– Isaiah 41:10

Daily Devotion

The favor of God enables and endorses you to beat the odds. When you are with God, no matter how outmanned or outgunned you are in any situation, you are still with the majority if you're with God. One of my favorite passages in the Bible is in 1 Kings 18.

As famine strikes the land, Elijah looks to face off against the prophets of Baal. Sadly, Elijah's side, the people of Israel, fell prey to poor leadership and were worshiping idols. Outnumbered 850 to 1, Elijah challenges the false prophets to a duel anyway.

"Let's see whose God is real!"

Elijah presents a challenge to the enemy: he will make a sacrifice to God and the prophets of Baal will do the same to their god. Whichever God shows up will be the God Israel will worship from now on. This contest required no faith for anyone watching. All they would need to do is watch the lonely prophet of God make a stand.

Maybe you feel like you are in a hopeless situation. Do you feel outnumbered and all alone? Perhaps the doctor said the fearful word *cancer*. Maybe your spouse said the crushing word *divorce*. Does your addiction seem too strong? Does your job look like a dead-end?

When we find God's favor at work, we see the situation can shift in a second.

After the prophets of Baal failed, it was Elijah's turn. Now, if God didn't show up, Elijah was dead meat. And although he knew the odds, his prayer was confident and his calling was sure. In fact, Elijah was so sure, he soaked the wood for his sacrifice with water before calling out to his God,

"God, show them you're the One true God, answer me by fire."

Suddenly, fire fell from heaven and completely consumed the offering, soaking wet wood and all. At the sight of this miracle, the people fell on their faces and said, "The Lord, He is God." (**1 Kings 18:39**).

God showed up and proved His power even when His servant looked outmatched with no hope for victory. God can do the same for you. But let me ask you, to where are you looking? At the circumstances, the odds, the enemy, or even your own strength? Or are you standing by faith in the favor of God flowing through you?

Ask Him to send a victory in your life, family, ministry, and profession. No matter how hopeless it looks, God is the victory. He said, "You are more than an overcomer."

God can burn up your problems and the circumstances surrounding you just like He burned up the sacrifice and everything surrounding it. No matter how worn out, weak, and wet your firewood, He can surprise you in a second and bring a fresh fire from Heaven to ignite your soul.

Brenda's Story — Part 1

My husband, Terry, was an amazing man. He loved me so much. When he was killed in a tree-cutting accident in our backyard a few years ago, my life turned upside down. The morning after his death, I didn't know what to do or where to turn. So, I went to the same place Terry went every day to meet with God.

As I sat in Terry's study, I cried out to God. "God, help me get through the painful days ahead. Guide me. Give me some words of encouragement. Give me hope in your Word." I flipped through the pages of the Bible and sensed the Lord directing me to the Psalms.

"But the book of Psalms is so long, God. Where do I look?" I said. As I turned pages, the Bible opened to Psalm 68, and I began to read. And just five verses later, something extraordinary happened. "[...] A father to the fatherless and a champion of widows." – Psalm 68:5 (CSB)

Just like that, I recognized, I was not alone. I was with the majority! God had not forgotten me. And He was promising to be my champion.

Brenda Moore serves on the front line at the Pellissippi Campus and has been the first face many people see when they stop by the offices for almost the last ten years. Brenda is an avid reader and proud grandmother of five grandchildren.

Faith Declaration

Today, I will walk with God. No matter what I face today, I will believe in victory, because God will win no matter what. God, the glory is Yours. I will face every enemy and stronghold because I am an overcomer. Your power will not be thwarted and Your favor will flow through me.

Question + Response

Think of all the times you walked with people through their
suffering. If you could revisit those times, how could you
have helped them see God's favor at work?

Prayers answered

Grateful for

How did God move?

───── Day Twenty-Six ─────

WHAT ARE THE ODDS?

"The Lord is good to those who wait for Him, to the person who seeks
Him. It is good that he waits silently for the salvation of the LORD."
– Lamentations 3:25-26

Daily Devotion

There have been times in my life when my situation looked
hopeless. But what looks impossible in the earthly is easy in
the heavenly. Like we saw yesterday, because of God's favor
at work, you are with the majority and mighty God.

In 2 Chronicles 20, we read another incredible story of
God's victory despite the odds. Israel has been divided into
two countries, Judah in the south and Israel in the north. In
Judah, King Jehoshaphat is a humble King seeking the heart
and favor of God. Jehoshaphat honors God, even though
many of his predecessors did not.

A coalition of the surrounding nations, with armies much
bigger and stronger than Judah's, unleashes an attack on
King Jehoshaphat and his people. The King responds by
seeking God's face and leading a prayer for all of his people.
He calls out,

**"Lord, we have no hope with this vast army marching
against us. Help!"**

How many of us in his position would have given up and
surrendered? How many of us would look to see God's favor
at work before giving into the hopelessness of this situation?

I love this part. God responds to the King, "The battle is mine, stand and watch." And what happens next is incredible! Jehoshaphat tells the people, "Believe in the Lord your God and you will win." And with everyone gathered on the battlefield, God's people don't make a battle cry or attack. Instead they sing and worship. They give thanks to the Lord for what He is *about* to do.

Read that last sentence again. What amazing faith! When the people of Judah finally step on the battlefield, the enemy soldiers, confused and panicked, turn on each other and annihilate themselves. It takes the Hebrews three days to pick up all the spoils left behind by their enemies.

I prayed for my little brother for thirty-five years. He was trapped in the worst kind of drug addiction. Everyone else gave up on ever hoping for him to get clean again. Finally, one time while visiting him in jail, God reached out of heaven, rescued, and restored my brother right in front me. No one believed it!

They said "as soon as he gets out, he'll be back on crack." Can I tell you five years later, he's still clean and faithfully following and serving Jesus! Never count God out! No matter what we face, God can and will overcome. Even when you don't see it, never give up hope.

God is always working!

If you've given up on a marriage or your business is not doing well, God's favor can still find you, rescue you, and restore you. God loves to win when the odds are not in your favor, because those are moments where His glory shines the brightest. And although I believe God meets us at the level of our expectations, He absolutely can and will exceed your expectations, if you believe.

Brenda's Story — Part 2

My husband Terry always took care of me. He even
took care of me in death through a life insurance policy.
Following his death, I was set to receive a large sum of
money from the policy. But during our thirty-seven years of
marriage, he always managed our finances, so I had no idea
how much money we had in the bank. I was struggling.

Was I supposed to tithe on this insurance money? Terry
never struggled. He never hesitated to give the church his
tithe. But I was resisting. It was going to be a significant
amount, and I had never handled our finances. Plus, I felt
like as long as I didn't spend the money, then it was okay.

God nudged my heart.

After one Sunday morning, I pulled Pastor Chris aside and
asked him to pray. I said, "God asked me to do something
big and I am afraid." Later in the afternoon, I went home
and wrote the check. When I gave it the following Sunday, I
had a huge smile and the burden was lifted off me.

A month later, I received a card in the mail from a friend. I
opened the card and curiously, out slid a check for $12,500.
I was stunned! What was this generous gift?! I could never
accept this much money. I was wrestling with God when He
clearly told me: "When God blesses you with a generous
gift, say thank you."

That evening while telling my sister the story, I picked up
the card and *another* check for $12,500 fell out. It must have
been stuck inside the envelope. I started crying and called
the friend who sent the checks.

The friend explained how her husband came home one day
and said, "God has prompted me to send money to help a
widow. Do we know any widows?"

"Yes!" she said, "Brenda is now a widow."

The family sent me two $12,500 checks and you better believe I did not hesitate to give generously this time around!

Faith Declaration

Today, I will walk in victory. God can overcome any and every problem I face. I will not fear or give up. With my God in charge, there is always hope. I will honor Him today with my lips and my life.

Question + Response

One of our values at Faith Promise is *We Give Generously*. Where are you and your family on the generosity journey?

Challenge: Ask God to show you some ways to be generous to someone who needs it.

Prayers answered

Grateful for

How did God move?

DREAM AGAIN

"Behold, I will do something new, now it will spring forth;
will you not be aware of it? I will even make a roadway
in the wilderness, rivers in the desert."
– Isaiah 43:19

Daily Devotion

For weeks now, we've talked about faith, favor, and our God the Waymaker. By now, hopefully you are prepared to see and receive God's favor and look for how is God already moving and working in every situation and circumstance.

Now is not the time to disqualify yourself from serving Him or discredit the miracles He is preparing. God is able. Don't talk yourself out of what He wants to do in your life. God has not disqualified you. Speak words of living water over yourself today, speak God's truth from Scripture, and stop speaking death.

What God calls you calls you out.

Just look at the life of Moses. Right from the start, his circumstances couldn't have been much worse. Moses was born in Egypt while the Hebrew people were enslaved. Pharaoh, fearing Israel, commanded all newborn Hebrew males to be killed. So, Moses' broken-hearted mother set him adrift in the Nile River rather than turning him over to be killed.

But if we look closely, God's favor was already at work in Moses' life. An Egyptian princess discovers the baby drifting in the reeds and adopts him. Moses grows up in the palace, living in the luxury of the Egyptians, while never losing his Hebrew heritage.

Still, the Bible describes Moses' anguish as he watches the Egyptian beat and work his people mercilessly. One day, he decides to take matters into his own hands and kill an Egyptian who was beating a Hebrew.

Moses thought his actions would earn him respect, but instead they only brought isolation. The Egyptians turn against him and his own people refuse to accept him. So, he runs away as a fugitive to Midian and many years pass. In that time, Moses becomes a shepherd, marries, and raises children.

His dream of rescuing the Hebrew people is gone, lost in the desert sand.

Have your dreams gone to Midian—forgotten, laid to rest, with no hope of return? Maybe it's time to dream again. Maybe it's time to look and see God's favor already at work in the dream you left behind or forgot.

Forty years after the incident in Egypt, God shows up to Moses and invites Him to dream again of freedom for God's people. And how does Moses respond? "You've got the wrong guy, God."

He immediately disqualifies himself with excuses. But let's be real, many of us do the same thing when God brings back to our attention long lost or forgotten dreams of His for our lives. Is it because excuses are easier than experiencing another disappointment?

Let me give you a word from heaven. God knows where you are and He is inviting you to dream again and to remember

His calling, hope, and vision for your life. He adopted you, loves you, and has amazing plans for your future.

Candis' Story

I was a good student and breezed through high school with A's. But, I always dreamed of graduating from college. And when I began college, my plan was to become a teacher.

Soon after marrying my husband, Jeff, I transferred to a school closer to where we lived and after two years, changed my major without finishing my associate degree. Then, I transferred and changed my major again.

In my fourth year of college, we found out we were pregnant, and although we were excited to become parents, things were no longer going as planned. In 2007, I decided to give up on my dream. Then, one summer day in 2009, while playing with our son, Malachi, God resurrected my dream and whispered to me.

"I want Malachi to know that he can do hard things. I want Malachi to know that he can go to college. That he can graduate."

I was going back to school and I was going to finish. I wasn't sure what to do next, but I knew God was working. So that fall I resumed online classes. Only this time, I went to God in prayer first.

I asked God to reveal my major and His calling for my life. I was only two years away from finishing a degree in Psychology and God gifted me to help people through difficult circumstances so I sensed God pointing me in this direction.

A few months later, I was pregnant again. But this time I did not quit, and in 2011, the dream came true and I graduated college. After graduating, it was clear God wanted me to use my gifts to counsel others. And seven years after my journey started, I was able to graduate with a master's degree in counseling!

We all have dreams.

What dreams have you set aside? Ask God about those dreams. Maybe He is already working and leading you toward the steps you need to take to fulfill those long-abandoned dreams and dream again.

Candis Cochran is one of Faith Promise's licensed staff counselors. Her husband, Jeff, serves on staff as the Farragut Groups and Missions Pastor. They each find new and creative ways to advance God's Kingdom every day.

Faith Declaration

I believe God is doing something new. I will find favor and look for the ways God is already moving and at work in my life and the lives of those around me. God is inviting me to dream again and find His favor already at work. God has plans and a purpose for my life, and I will walk in His blessings and favor.

Question + Response

What would dreaming again look like in your life?

_____

_____

_____

_____

Who does God want you to speak life into right now? Take a
moment right now to encourage them with a life-giving call,
text, or message.

_____

_____

_____

_____

Prayers answered

Grateful for

How did God move?

JEHOVAH-JIREH

"And my God will supply all your needs
according to His riches in glory in Christ Jesus."
– Philippians 4:19

Daily Devotion

Let's take a trip back in time to the Stephens' household thirty-some years ago in southwest Louisiana. I remember opening the door to the refrigerator. Empty. Not even a box of baking soda in the back. In the freezer, nothing but ice. The pantry shelves, empty. Bank account, nothing but zeroes.

Meanwhile, my son Micah needs surgery and we have no insurance or money to pay for the surgery. Can I be real with you? I felt like a failure.

I wasn't providing for my family. I was a pastor of a church plant making $16,000 a year and Michele and I were renting a little house with Faith, Zac, and Micah. But I didn't give up on God. I had faith enough to make this request.

"God, I need you to move."

There was a widow in Israel who faced a similar situation. Her husband provided throughout their life, but after he died, she was left with nothing. The widow was so deep in debt that when the collectors showed up, they wanted to take her two sons as payment. There was no way out.

Then Elisha shows up. She tells him of her impossible situation, and he asks her this question, "What do you have in the house?" She was in the same position we were when in southwest Louisiana. Empty shelves.

"I have nothing," she says, "But maybe a drop of oil."

Never discount the small things you have because that may be what the Lord uses to fuel His favor. Your resources may be little or dried up, but remember all the way back from Day 1: our Source has unlimited blessings and favor to offer.

The prophet tells her to bring him empty jars. The widow obeys by faith. Elisha continues, "Now pour the oil from the small jar into the larger vessels, keep pouring until all the jars are full." And God keeps the oil flowing until there are no more jars. "Now, sell the oil and pay your creditors and live on the rest."

When God pours out favor, there will be enough to fill you and live on!

Back to Jennings, Louisiana. I kept my faith. And a couple of days later, we opened our minivan door to find a backseat full of groceries. Then, a friend of a friend covered the entire cost of Micah's surgery. God *will* provide. Just like the overflowing oil, you *can* trust Him to meet your need.

Our God is Jehovah-Jireh and our Source to look to first, not last.

Mike's Story

"Dad, can I have a bicycle?" asked Ashley, our oldest daughter.

151

I smiled at her as we sat on the front porch that warm spring afternoon. How could you not want to bless such an adorable child with such a simple request? But there was a problem. Money was tight. As much as I wanted to tell her yes, I had to say no. Kandice and I had seen God provide in many ways throughout our life, so we decided to use the moment to teach Ashley about God's provision.

We shared with Ashley how God can provide in many miraculous ways and encouraged her to pray and ask God for a bicycle. To our surprise, she immediately closed her eyes and went silent. When she opened her eyes, she looked up into the clouds.

"What are you looking for, Ashley?"

"I just asked God for my bicycle."

Her mother and I tried to hold back our laughter and explained God would probably not drop a bicycle from out of the sky. He answers prayers differently, we said.

A couple of days later, we visited Kandice's parents. When we arrived, Kandice's dad, Grandpa Paul, met us in the driveway and asked me to come with him. We walked across the street, and he opened his neighbor's garage. When he opened that garage door, it was as if time stopped and all the angels of Heaven were shining spotlights onto the most beautiful girl's bicycle. It was perfect! The glittery paint, the silver and purple streamers sticking out from each side of the handlebars, the silver horn, and, of course, training wheels.

He told me that his neighbor was selling the bicycle in a garage sale the next morning, but he wanted my permission to purchase the bike for Ashley. Grandpa Paul had no idea that days earlier, Ashley had prayed and asked God to give her a bicycle. Well, you guessed it, Ashley got her bike and we all learned a lesson that day.

God is our Provider and Source! Maybe you need to have the faith of a child. Go ahead, ASK HIM, then step off your porch and look up to see God's favor at work!

As you read on Day 15, Mike Baker is the North Knox Campus Pastor and leads faithfully on the Faith Promise staff, along with his wife, Kandice, who is the fpKIDS Pastor at North Knox.

Faith Declaration

Today, I declare by faith that my God can. There is no problem I will face today that He hasn't already planned a way out. I will not give up hope. I will turn to God first in faith, especially if I face problems bigger than I am.

Question + Response

If you stopped posing and keeping yourself from being real with God, what would be revealed as your deepest need?

Prayers answered

Grateful for

How did God move?

JEHOVAH-RAPHA

"When He [Jesus] went ashore, He saw a large crowd,
and felt compassion for them and healed their sick."
– Matthew 14:14

Daily Devotion

We pray to the Lord for many things. We trust God will move in many ways. But honestly, some prayers feel harder than others. And physical healing is often the most difficult miracle to believe God will fulfill.

Sure, we read story after story in the Bible and we might even hear people share stories of God's miraculous touch. But many of us don't believe He can do it for us.

Listen Promisor, I have seen God move when there was no other way. I've seen doctors shocked by what they see, or no longer see, on an X-ray. I have seen people get to the surgery table only for the doctors to be blown away because the cancer they were meant to operate on is miraculously gone. God does the unexplainable and moves in the supernatural.

God can heal!

One of my favorite healing stories is in the Bible in 2 Kings 5. Naaman was a decorated hero and captain of an enemy's army. But Naaman got sick. His body became infected with a skin disease called leprosy.

However, one of his servants was a young girl from Israel who shared some insider info with Naaman. In her homeland, there was a prophet named Elisha and he was known as a healer.

So, Naaman heads to Israel and makes his way to Elisha's house. But the prophet does not even leave his living room to greet Naaman, instead He sends a servant out with this message: "Go to the Jordan river and dip seven times."

Naaman was insulted. He turned around and left in a huff. Then, one of his servants talks some sense into him asking, "If he asked you to do some great feat you would have done it, why not do this?"

Isn't that how we think? If I do something great for God, then He will move. Then He will help me. But God does not always work like we think He should. God moves by grace, and not by our efforts. There is no *quid pro quo* with God.

It's all a gift. It's all grace and mercy.

So Naaman dips seven times and after the seventh time, he is healed! By the way, God can still heal.

My daughter, Faith, is still daddy's little girl. So, it was devastating to watch her struggle when her doctor said, "If you want kids, start the adoption process. It's your only hope."

But she believed God could intervene. So, during a Heart for the Harvest weekend at Faith Promise, she came forward and was surrounded by people who began praying with outstretched hands. And you know what happened?

God moved.

Today, she is the mother of a beautiful daughter, Bella Grace. Don't give up hope for your healing or your miracle. Can you see? God's favor is at work! Are you looking? While doctors practice medicine, and we should absolutely use their expertise, only God—Jehovah Rapha—has the power to heal.

Chad's Story

Growing up, I never went to church and definitely never read the Bible. But I did smoke my first joint during Christmas when I was twelve years old, if that counts.

The next eighteen years of my life was a dark journey. I was a liar. A horrible husband. A dead beat father. And a junkie. Sometimes I spent $600 a week on meth. Do you know what people said about me?

"There is no hope for him. Chad Funk will always be a drug addict."

One day I came home from work and took a bunch of sleeping pills and drank a bottle of vodka. I was going to end my life because it was the only way I felt I would be free from addiction. My wife found me and called the police.

In front of my family and neighbors, I was handcuffed and led away to be put into a psychiatric ward. I was on a constant suicide watch. Then, a miracle happened.

One night I invited Jesus into my heart. I asked him to be my Lord and to take what I destroyed and restore it. When I prayed that night, I was not even sure if I believed or if it was possible for Jesus to fix my mess.

But the next day I woke up and I was something new.

Jesus radically healed me! Something inside me was

changed and my eternity was changed, as well. When I walked out of the rehabilitation center, I never looked back.

God can do abundantly more than we ask or think. If God can entirely deliver me from my drug addiction, what can't He deliver you from?

Thirteen years later, I have never gone back. He gives me victory and showers me with favor every day in the throne room of grace.

Chad Funk and his wife, Brandi, have been a part of Faith Promise for many years. He serves on staff as the fpKIDS Elementary Pastor for the Pellissippi Campus.

Faith Declaration

Today, I will believe God for any miracle I need. My God has no limits and I have full faith in Him. No matter what the doctor or anyone else says, I'll give God the last word in my life. No matter what the report says, my Maker can heal me and make me whole. I will serve Him. I trust God with my today and my eternity.

Question + Response

Who in your circle is living with a physical need only God
can heal?

_____

_____

_____

_____

Spend a few minutes journaling some specific prayers for
healing.

_____

_____

_____

_____

Prayers answered

Grateful for

How did God move?

JEHOVAH-SABAOTH

"Show me a sign for good, that those who hate me may see it and be
ashamed, because You, O LORD, have helped me and comforted me."
– Psalm 86:17

Daily Devotion

When I was in school, I lived in fear. I dealt with bullies
all the time. I was small for my age and didn't hit a growth
spurt until after high school. This made me an easy target.
Today, bullying is a bigger and more complicated problem
than ever. Girls and boys now get bullied in person and on
the Internet. And far too many teenagers live in fear and
anxiety from physical, verbal, and emotional abuse.

I love what the psalmist says in **Psalm 86:17:**

> **"Show me a sign for good [favor], that those
> who hate me [bullies] may see it and be ashamed."**

I believe God still does this for His children. He can shame
the bullies in your life and prove His favor is on you and at
work all around you. When Micah was young, he played
Pee-Wee football. One kid on the team was bigger, and
at practice, he constantly bullied Micah. But, instead of
confronting the bully, Micah was tempted to quit playing on
the team and in a game he loved. Does this sound familiar?

Well, I made Micah go back to practice and face his bully
because if he let this bully make him quit, it might become a
habit. Micah confronted his bully and the boy backed down,

never to bother him again. Don't let Satan or any other bully keep you from all God's desires for you. Face them!

> **"Submit therefore to God. Resist the devil**
> **and he will flee from you."**
> **– James 4:7**

Sure, people can be bullies sometimes, but Satan is the ultimate bully. And our enemy would like nothing more than to see you cower in fear and miss all God is planning for you. If we truly believe that "greater is He who is in us than he that is in the world," then we need to start living like God's favor is already at work.

We have the real people's champion! Someone the prophet Isaiah calls the "Dread Champion." King Jesus is the champion of all those who are weak and defenseless. And He will astonish and confound any bully in your life. So there is no reason to fear.

> **"[...] If God is for us, who can ever be against us?"**
> **– Romans 8:31 (NLT)**

One of the many names of God we find in the Old Testament is Jehovah-Sabaoth, or the "Lord of Hosts" or "Armies." So, you can confidently rest, run, and bask in His favor and protection on your life. Look and see God's favor is a force ready to fight and help you face any bully in your life.

Faith Declaration

Today, I will not be bullied by the enemy. God will confound my enemies with His favor in my life. I will walk in God's plan for me today. Because God is with me, I am more than an overcomer and I will not fear anyone.

Question + Response

What relationships do you have where you need God's
confidence and healing?

_____

_____

_____

_____

What step will you take today to bring restoration to that
relationship?

_____

_____

_____

_____

Psalm 23:5 says that God has prepared a table in the presence of your enemies.

Prayers answered

Grateful for

How did God move?

JEHOVAH-SHAMMAH

"Let the favor of the Lord our God be upon us; and confirm for us the
work of our hands; yes, confirm the work of our hands."
– Psalm 90:17

Daily Devotion

As we look to wrap up this incredible month in *Finding
Favor,* it is truly my prayer you are now able to see God's
blessings and favor at work in every day and every way of
your life.

When things are going great, and when things are terrible.

When everyone is on your side, and when no one is on your
side.

Even if it looks unlikely or even impossible, I pray you will
find God's favor at work.

Before you close this book, take a look back through your
prayer journal and celebrate the ways you can already see
God's favor at work. If there are still areas where you desire
to see God's favor more clearly, continue to pray. If you have
your own prayer journal or personal growth plan, transfer
these prayer requests and dreams over so you can continue
to talk with God and ask to see Him make those dreams
become reality.

We all have dreams and visions buried deep in our hearts.

It's easy to punt our dreams, put them on the back burner, or just plain forget about them. Forgotten dreams lead believers to settle for "good enough," missing the potential God placed in each of us. Our God is abundant, and His force of favor can take you further than you think.

Nehemiah didn't lose his dream. He served as the cup-bearer to the King of Babylon; a cabinet-level position. But Nehemiah's heart was with his Jewish brothers and sisters still in Jerusalem.

One day, when some friends from Jerusalem come for a visit, they share terrible news. The city walls are torn down, the gates burn, and depression is overwhelming the hearts of the Hebrews.

Nehemiah was broken-hearted. But what could he do?

He's just too far away, maybe there's nothing he can do. Maybe God will send someone else to help rebuild the wall and the hearts of the people of God. Or maybe he will see God's favor and begin to believe God can use him.

Thankfully, Nehemiah chose to believe God for favor. After a time of prayer, God cleared the way and Nehemiah walked with the full confidence of Heaven.

Nehemiah asks the King for leave to go to Jerusalem. He will rebuild the walls. But, Nehemiah doesn't stop there. He is bold! He asks the King for resources, a passport, and support for anything else he needs. And what happened?

The King gave him everything he needed.

Fifty-two days later, Nehemiah finishes the impossible construction project and stacks the last brick of the completely rebuilt wall. Nehemiah didn't have a contractor's license or the skills to undertake the project. What he did have was the favor of God. And when he trusted God's favor, God confirmed the work of his hands.

Faith Promise faces multiple mountains, but God's favor is on our church. He carries us past every problem and wall, and into every opportunity. When we moved from Oak Ridge to Pellissippi, we could not afford it. But we moved by faith.

Many people thought we were crazy. But today we are thousands of Promisors strong across ten campuses and growing! We still feel the favor of God. Remember how that room looked last year during our 25th anniversary celebration?

Regardless of any disease or division, the economy or unemployment, and most certainly regardless of who is in the White House—only the One who sits on the Throne of Heaven matters. Man, I am so glad to be a part of this church. Our future has never looked brighter.

If you want to find favor, look and see how God's favor is already at work in your life and walk in it. Then watch as God confirms the work of our hands for His glory.

Faith Declaration

We will walk with the force of favor, propelling us further and faster than we could ever go on our own. God will open up the flow of His favor and pave the way for us to bring Him greater glory. We will not back down from any challenge because God is with us.

Question + Response

Read Joshua 4:1-24.

In this passage, we read that the Israelites made stones into memorials so they could remember the great things God had done. On the next page, take a few minutes to record some revelations on your stones.

What is God doing in your life right now?

_____

_____

_____

_____

_____

_____

_____

What has God revealed
to you in your Journey so far?
(Write any words, thoughts, and/or verses below)

word of the year

Prayers answered

Grateful for

How did God move?

Who can you help to discover the same favor you've found over these 31 days?

...Where you live? (Your family members or neighbors)

...Where you work? (Your co-workers or clients)

...Where you study? (Your classmates, teachers, or students)

...Where you shop or eat? (Your cashier or server)

...Where you play? (Your teammates or friends)